MARC CHAGALL

Marc

Chagall

HOWARD GREENFELD

*With reproductions of the artist's work
in color and black and white*

Follett Publishing Company

Chicago   New York

Title page: from *My Life*, Plate 17, *Self-Portrait* (Drypoint)

The Art Institute of Chicago

Library of Congress Catalog Card Number: 68-10479

*Copyright © 1967, by Howard Greenfeld. All rights
reserved. No portion of this book may be reproduced
in any form without written permission from the publisher.
Manufactured in the United States of America.
Published simultaneously in Canada by The Ryerson Press, Toronto.*

*Follett Publishing Company
1010 West Washington Boulevard
Chicago, Illinois 60607*

*First Printing
T/L 5523*

This book is dedicated, with love, to
Ann, my wife
My parents
and
Anne, my niece

PREFACE

One of the first paintings I ever saw—I had stood before many, but had actually *seen* few—was that of a violinist on a roof. I was very young then, but I knew that everything was wrong. The violinist's colors were wrong—he had a green face; he was much too big for the town in the background; his shoes were of different colors and his mouth was impossibly crooked.

Yet of all the pictures I had been taken to see, that was the one I remembered. It made no sense, but I had been indescribably happy looking at it and remembering it.

It was a painting by Marc Chagall, one of the most important and most popular painters of our time. At the time, I never dreamed that I would meet the man whose painting had given me such happiness. Yet, several years ago I found

7

myself in Berne, Switzerland, about to meet the great Chagall. We had an appointment at the home of his daughter, Ida. As I walked up the stairs to the front door, I was frightened. Not only was I afraid to meet this creative genius, but I couldn't even speak to him in English, a language he hardly knew, or in French, a language I hardly knew.

A few moments after being let into the home and shown to the living room, I was no longer afraid. Marc Chagall was carelessly playing with his small grandchildren as I timidly entered the room. I will never forget his warmth, the love that radiated from him. Clearly, he was not a man to fear. To me, he looked like a combination of Harpo Marx and Charlie Chaplin. But there was something special about him, something far deeper—a questioning, an intelligence, a sensitivity. . . . There was humor in his face, but there was also sadness and understanding and a concern for all living creatures.

I enjoyed that evening and left exhilarated.

I saw Chagall several times after that—with his warm and lovely wife Vava in their sun-drenched home in Vence, near the French Riviera; in Paris where they live in a house overlooking the timelessly enchanted Seine; in New York, where he walked the streets with the curiosity of a child and the wisdom of an artist; in Waltham, Massachusetts, at Brandeis University, when he modestly accepted an honorary degree, far more interested in the vitality of the students than in his own "importance."

Each meeting has been a valued experience for me, and I have been deeply impressed by his modesty, his dedication to his work, his lack of pretension (I remember his insisting I take off my freshly pressed shirt and jacket in exchange for an old checked flannel shirt of his to put me more at ease at one of our meetings), his standards of excellence, and his integrity.

This book will answer several questions: Who is he? Where was he born? How did he become a painter? Important as these facts are, the most important thing about Chagall is his painting. To live, we all need nourishment; not only food and fresh air, but beauty as well. It feeds us and makes us grow. To see, to feel the paintings of Chagall is also a form of nourishment. It is in Chagall's work that his greatness and importance lie. The joy or the sadness we experience when looking at his art constitutes a wealth we can all share.

His story begins in Vitebsk, the provincial Russian town in which Chagall was born. A large and recurring part of his work contains memories and dreams of his childhood there. Marc Chagall was born in Vitebsk, but we must be careful where we place the emphasis in such a sentence. *Marc Chagall* was born in Vitebsk, it must read, for that small Russian town existed for many and many were born there. But it took Chagall's genius to transform that one small town into something of beauty for all of us. The evidence for this is found in his paintings. It is my sincere hope that the readers of this book will go on to see, to enjoy, and to be enriched by the works of this modern master.

Very many people have helped me, in one way or another, in writing this book. I thank them all. But I would especially like to thank Mrs. Freda Barry Brown and Mary Scheinman, for their unusual kindness and generosity when I needed both.

H.G.

MARC CHAGALL

THE BOY AND THE VILLAGE

The young boy with the blond curly hair and the flashing blue eyes wandered lazily, dreamily through the streets of the town. In his hand was a piece of bread and butter. From time to time, he absentmindedly chewed on the bread as he looked about him.

It had been raining, and the streets were dotted with puddles and splattered with mud, for few of them were paved.

He looked up at the gray sky, and his eyes passed over the pear-domed church towers. It was a town of rooftops and chimneys and steeples. His eyes followed the ripples in the corrugated iron roofs.

He kept walking up and down the narrow streets, past the many synagogues and the beautiful fifteenth-century cathedral, past the stores—there seemed to be hundreds of tailors—and the workshops and the small factories.

There was the railway station and then the river Dvina, brown with mud. He paused at the bridge and then crossed it, still nibbling at the bread and looking about him.

Away from the center of the town, he found the simple houses—frame cabins and well-built painted log houses, and sturdier stone houses. Behind the houses, there were gardens and backyards. In one, a scrawny chicken was scratching for worms.

In the streets, talking, were peasant women in head-scarves and men in Russian blouses and peaked caps.

He passed the gray wooden buildings and the jagged wooden fences.

A bearded rabbi walked solemnly by; a beggar, weighed down by a heavy sack, leaned against a yellow stone building.

Children ran home from the cheder, the Hebrew elementary school, and hens strutted on the roofs.

Dusk settled over the city, and the sweet stars came into the sky.

Bread and butter no longer in his hands, the boy went home.

All he had seen had become magical through his eyes. The town was Vitebsk, population about 50,000, the district capital of the province of the same name, on the Russo-

Polish border. The boy was Marc Chagall, and he would some day become one of the most important painters of the twentieth century.

The Chagall household was a poor one. Zahar Chagall, a tall, thin bearded man, arose each morning at six o'clock. He dressed and went to the synagogue to say his daily prayers. This done, he would return home, prepare the samovar and drink his tea. Ahead of him lay a long, hard day of work at the warehouse where, hour after hour, he lugged heavy barrels of salted herring. He had worked for Jachnine the herring dealer for many years, rolling the barrels around the warehouse, showing them to potential customers and finally delivering them to the railway station.

Every evening he would come home, his clothing soiled with herring brine, a dull red handkerchief showing from one of his pockets. In his gray-blue eyes, sadness and fatigue. Often he would reach into his pockets, take out sweet cakes and frosted pears and give them to his children. But he rarely spoke to them, and when he did, it was to quote a religious passage or give a piece of advice. Zahar Chagall's life had been a hard one. In Vitebsk, possibilities for Jews were limited, and right after finishing cheder, he was apprenticed to the herring dealer. His father had hoped he might become a clerk, but he never even reached that position.

From *My Life,* Plate 10, *Dining Room* (Drypoint)
The Art Institute of Chicago

It was Mama Chagall who led the family and took over from her husband; more often than not, he was fast asleep, gently snoring, before the dinner was over. She was a woman of great dignity and greater energy. Not only did she provide love and guidance to her own children—Marc, Aniuta, David, Zina, Lisa, Manya, Rosa, Maroussia and Rachel (who died in infancy)—but she also mothered her

16

many sisters. In addition, this kindly, alert woman managed a small shop where she sold herring, flour, sugar, and spices.

Marc had been born in 1887; he was her pride and joy, her favorite. In fact, he was everyone's favorite. The entire family—and it was a large one—adored the dreamy-eyed boy. Marc, for his part, had two favorites: his grandfather, a butcher at the country town of Lyozno, near Vitebsk, whom the young boy would joyfully visit in the summer, even forgiving him the horrors of the slaughterhouse; and Uncle Neuch, who would ride out to the country, with Marc in his cart, to buy cattle from the peasants, and then return home to play the violin—like a cobbler.

There were other uncles, a half dozen or more: Uncle Leiba, Uncle Judah, Uncle Israel, Uncle Zussy, a hairdresser in Lyozno.... And many aunts: Aunt Mariassja, the pale one, and Aunt Relly whose nose was like a pickle, and Aunt Moussia, Aunt Gouttja, Aunt Chaja....

They all loved little Marc—and they all agreed that there was something special about him.

When the time came, Marc was sent to study in the cheder, which he attended for eight years. The chief subjects were Hebrew characters and language and the Bible. Biblical knowledge was of great importance in the education of all Jewish boys and in time Marc became as familiar with the characters of the Bible as he was with those he met in the streets of Vitebsk. To him they were living, breathing people. His teachers were three rabbis. One of them, Rabbi Djatkine, a kindly, intelligent man, paid special attention to young Marc. It was with Rabbi Djatkine that the boy first studied the Talmud, the book of Jewish law and tradition. From him, too, he learned by heart the important sermons which he proudly recited to his parents. In his spare time, he took violin lessons and singing lessons, helping out the cantor in the synagogue.

As soon as he finished his studies at the cheder, Marc entered the public school where he remained for six years. Though he worked hard, he was not a good pupil: he was, as he had always been, a dreamer. But the time had come when he had to decide what to do with his life. One thing he knew: he would do anything to avoid the life of drudgery which his father had led. Nor would he be happy as a butcher or hairdresser or sacristan of a synagogue. There were, unfortunately, few choices for a Jewish boy in Vitebsk.

One day, in his drawing class, a fellow pupil brought in a charcoal drawing he had done. It was a detailed copy of a drawing that had appeared in a popular illustrated magazine, *Niva*.

Marc looked at it with envy. "Did you do that?" he asked the boy, stuttering.

From *Dead Souls* by Gogol, Plate 80 (Etching and Drypoint)
The Art Institute of Chicago

The boy proudly admitted that he had.

If he could do it, so could I, thought Marc. As soon as the class ended, he ran to the library. Going through the illustrated books and magazines to find a subject to copy, he found a portrait of a Russian composer, Anton Rubinstein, that fascinated him. He set to work and produced a copy of it every bit as good as the one done by the boy in his class. He then found other drawings to copy, and each day after school would enthusiastically work at his newfound skill. He loved doing it and soon brought the drawings home where he hung them on the walls of his room.

Every day he would look at them, admire them, and then decide to do even better ones. He was enjoying himself as he never had before. Then, one day, he had a visit from a school friend. The friend looked at the walls and turned to Marc. With surprise, he said: "Say! You're a real artist, aren't you?"

TO BE AN ARTIST

"You're a real artist . . . a real artist . . . a real artist. . . ."

His friend's words kept racing through his mind. He had never dared use such a word, think of such a thing. He knew he would never be happy with the kind of life his father had; nor, he felt, would he be happy as a clerk or an accountant. "An artist." It was true that he had looked for a language of his own, a language different from words, through which to express his thoughts, his ideas, his feelings —his love and his dreams. For a while, he had wanted to be a great singer, like the cantor in the synagogue; or even, perhaps, a violinist, like the fiddlers of Vitebsk who played their sweet and sad melodies in the town. But, no—he would be an artist. That was how he could best make himself known and heard and understood.

He was always good in drawing class; only geometry and drawing had interested him in school. He spent the rest of the time staring out the window, dreaming and seeing things his own way. If he could be a painter, he could show those things that haunted him—the flowers, oil lamps, samovars; the soft-eyed cows, the flickering candles, the people of Vitebsk, fiddlers and rabbis and peasants.

"You're a real artist."

But what would his mother say, and his father, and all the uncles and aunts? The Jews of Vitebsk paid strict attention to the Second Commandment: "Thou shalt not make unto thee any graven images, or any likeness of any thing that is in heaven above or that is in the earth beneath or that is in the water beneath the earth." Because of this Commandment, religious Jews did not paint, there was no tradition of painting. Indeed, the very few Jews who did paint lived in the big cities, and they lived more actively among non-Jews. But in Vitebsk, even the rich and worldly Jews only had prints portraying religious personalities or festivals in their homes.

There was no doubt that it would be difficult to explain to his mother just why he wanted to be an artist, why he felt the need to show things the way *he* saw them, why he wanted so badly to create beauty out of colors and shapes. He couldn't explain this to himself, but he knew he had to

From *My Life*, Plate 2, *Mother and Son* (Drypoint)
The Art Institute of Chicago

do something about it. He remembered the sign he had so often seen in the town: Artist Pen's School of Painting and Design. It was there that he had to go, to study and learn his art. But how could he convince his mother, and how could he get her to take him to see Artist Pen?

One day, he felt the time had come to bring up the subject. It was morning. His mother was alone, putting the bread in the oven. Marc watched her nervously; then, suddenly, he went up to her, took her by her flour-smeared elbow, and said: "Mama, I want to be a painter."

Startled, his mother almost dropped the bread pan. So this was it, this was what her boy wanted. It couldn't be . . . a painter. What would the family say? How would he ever make a living, why didn't he want something solid and respectable?

The boy begged and pleaded with her, told her about Pen's school and how he wanted her to take him there. He insisted that he just couldn't be a clerk or an accountant. Couldn't she understand?

No, she was too upset to understand, or at least to say she did. It was terrible; he simply couldn't do such a thing. The only thing for her to do was to discuss it with the family. Maybe they could make her understand. . . .

The rest of the family, of course, was even more horri-

24

fied than she had been. On hearing that Marc was actually drawing human figures, Uncle Israel in Lyozno even refused to shake hands with him. But Marc was so determined and stubborn. . . . Finally, it was Uncle Pissarevsky who gave her the courage to do what she knew she would have to do. "If he has talent, he should try." That's what Uncle Pissarevsky said—he was the most modern and up-to-date of the family. He even knew the works of the important Russian painters and admired them. In a way, it seemed that he was proud of his great-nephew's decision.

So it was decided. Marc and his mother were to go to see Artist Pen, to ask him if the boy had any talent, to find out if he could possibly teach him to be a painter. With five rubles—the cost of a month's lessons—that had been given him by his father, in his pockets, with a roll of tattered sketches in his hand, Marc set off, his mother nervously trailing behind. The streetcar that took them down toward the cathedral seemed so slow, but finally, there it was—a large blue sign, with white lettering, swaying gently in the breeze: ARTIST PEN'S SCHOOL OF PAINTING AND DESIGN. It was really a sign like any other, like the one for the tobacco shop or the bakery or the tailor or the butcher. But to Marc it seemed different, for the blue was the blue of the sky.

Trembling with excitement, Marc entered the building with his mother. As they slowly climbed the stairs, he smelled the clean, clear smell of the paint. Along the stairway, on both sides, were portraits. The faces of important people were permanently placed on canvas. It wasn't the kind of painting that Marc had dreamed of doing, but . . .

Timidly, they stood at the door to the studio and then entered. From floor to ceiling, the place was covered with paintings; on the floor, too, were piles of papers and sketches and drawings. Only the ceiling itself had no paintings on it; in their place were gigantic cobwebs. Here and there, throughout the room, Greek plaster heads, arms, legs, and ornaments, white objects all covered with dust. It was awful, but it was beautiful too.

Marc and his mother stood alone in the empty studio. Not a sign of life anywhere. The worried woman looked around the room, her eyes going from painting to painting. Finally she turned to her son: "Well, Marc . . . you see, you'll never be able to do things like that. Let's go home."

Never do things like that, Marc thought. Of course not. He knew already that this Artist Pen, Yehuda Pen, was not the kind of painter he would or could ever be. This could not be his way and he knew it; but he would paint, he knew he must—and in a language other than Pen's. Nonetheless, he could learn something from Pen, and it was Yehuda Pen who would decide whether or not he was qualified to study painting.

26

Of course, it was frightening. What if Pen told his mother he had no talent, that it would be a waste of time? Marc knew this was untrue, but what if Pen were in a bad mood? Even worse, what if Pen, sensing that Marc would never adapt to his own style, were angry and thus told his mother that there was no hope? Marc Chagall felt that, for the moment at least, his whole future, his whole life depended on Yehuda Pen.

It seemed like an endless wait, but Pen finally arrived. He entered the door, crossed the room, and bowed casually to his prospective pupil's mother. He was a short man, with a blond pointed goatee.

"What can I do for you?" he said.

Hesitatingly, Marc's mother spoke. "Well, I don't know . . . he wants to be a painter. . . . He's crazy." She looked at her son's anxious eyes, and then turned back to Pen. "But please look at his drawings. If he has any talent, it would be worthwhile for him to take lessons. If he hasn't . . ." She turned to Marc. "Come, my son, we're going home."

Marc looked at his mother and then, with determination, unrolled the torn drawings he had worked so hard on. Pen looked through them mechanically.

"Yes," he said slowly, carefully. "He has some ability."

It wasn't much, but it was all that Marc had wanted

From *My Life, Grandfather's House* (Drypoint)
Collection, The Museum of Modern Art, New York

to hear. Now his mother had to let him study with Pen. It was only a beginning, but it was a beginning.

So it was that Marc Chagall formally entered the world of art—and for this reason his lessons at Pen's were important. From Pen, he could learn some of the techniques, but he had been right when, as he walked up the narrow staircase to the studio that first day, he had sensed that his work would be completely different from Pen's. They were indeed expressing themselves in a different language. Pen saw his subjects much as a color photographer would; Marc's vision was his own personal one, as it always would be, and he could not merely reproduce. His teacher's paintings were cold and formal, while his own were warm and personal. Though he certainly did not yet dare to use color as he would in later years, he did have the courage to use violet in his paintings. This, instead of angering Pen, made him agree to teach his young pupil for nothing for a while. This is but one example of Pen's kindness. He was a good man, and Chagall was always to feel affection for him, but the teacher could do little to further the art of Chagall, and the young Marc studied with him for only a few months.

During his period at Pen's school, however, Marc was able to meet a new and different group of people and become friends with those who shared his own interest in the world of art. Most important of these was Victor Mekler. Victor was a sensitive boy, somewhat younger than Marc, from a wealthy family. After finishing school, he decided to become an artist and enrolled in Pen's school. He was drawn to Marc, and they soon became good friends. One day, Victor asked his friend to give him lessons, feeling there were things he could learn from Marc that he was unable to learn from Pen. Marc was delighted; it was an honor to be asked, and he enthusiastically agreed. However, this was to be an act of friendship, and he would take no money from Victor, though he badly needed it.

The two spent hours together, painting and talking, sharing their joy in their art. Day after day was spent either in Victor's home in Vitebsk or in his family's luxurious country home. After a while, Victor announced that he was going to continue his studies in Saint Petersburg and suggested that Marc come with him.

It was a marvelous idea, an exciting one, but it was a difficult decision for Marc to make. In a way, it was the final commitment to the world of art. In addition to his own painting, he had been for some time apprenticed to a photographer, A. Miestschaniff, as a retoucher. Though he hated the work, it promised a good, steady future. But security, a beautiful house, fine furniture—all these seemed very unimportant. He did know he could never be satisfied to be a

30

photographer or a retoucher, that his vision could never coin-
cide with that of a mere camera.

There were other problems, too. One of the most important was money. There was none at home and, in fact,
all his father could possibly give him was twenty-seven rubles
which certainly couldn't last very long in Saint Petersburg.
Then, too, all Jews needed a special permit to live in that
city. This permit was given to members of professions, to
their domestic servants and occasionally to workers employed
by them. One other way was possible—a merchant in a small
provincial town was allowed to delegate someone to do busi-
ness for him in Saint Petersburg. Through a friend of Marc's
father, the latter method was made possible since the elder
Chagall persuaded his friend, a businessman, to state that
Marc was commissioned to bring goods for him to and from
Saint Petersburg.

With Victor Mekler's urging and, in spite of the ob-
stacles placed before him, Marc decided to go to the capital.
It was a big step and a frightening one. He was shy and
afraid—he'd be alone in a strange city, and he'd be practi-
cally penniless. But his drive to become an artist was greater
than his fears. He knew he could never succeed in Vitebsk
—he was hemmed in there, unable to breathe the air he
needed in order to enlarge his art. He knew and understood
the struggles that awaited him as an artist. But he really had

no choice—only through art would he be able to fulfill himself. So it was that, in 1907, with a heavy heart but with a
sense of destiny, he set out for Saint Petersburg—on his way
to a new life.

Burning House (1913)
The Solomon R. Guggenheim Museum Collection

Over Vitebsk   Museum of Modern Art, New York

Le Repas Familial (The Family Meal)   Perls Galleries, New York

The Birthday · Museum of Modern Art, New York

SAINT PETERSBURG

When Marc Chagall arrived in the capital, Saint Petersburg was alive with excitement and change. The many minority groups who had come from all over Russia were beginning to assert themselves culturally, and their different arts and crafts and customs were enriching the life of the city. Contact with and influence from western Europe too was slowly but steadily growing.

However, upon his arrival, young Chagall was mainly concerned with the day-to-day difficulties of survival. His father's twenty-seven rubles did not, as he had known, last very long, and he was forced to work again as a retoucher for a photographer. For this, he was paid a bare minimum, just enough to pay for a meager amount of food. In fact, he was so often cold and hungry that his health failed, and he began to suffer from fainting spells.

Finding a place to live, too, was a problem, and Chagall never had a room of his own, and very seldom even a bed of his own. In the beginning, he shared a small room with an unruly sculptor. Then, he was forced to share a bed with a black-mustached workman, a kindly man who flattened himself against the wall to give the young painter more room in the bed. Later on there was a man whose snoring kept him up all night, and after that a drunken accordion player and his wife, and then a mysterious Persian.

But these struggles were worth it to the dedicated young man if he could only further his career. He would do anything to become a painter; most important of all, he had to go to the best possible school. Of course, the famous Academy was the best school in the city, but to enter it Chagall had to have a high school diploma. Since he had no such diploma, his best chance was at Baron Stieglitz's School of Applied Art. Since all pupils of the school were automatically given the necessary permits to stay in Saint Petersburg, Chagall went there as soon as he arrived in the city. For the entrance exam, he had to copy a plaster design—a vine stem with a bunch of grapes and many leaves. He worked hard on the drawing, and he liked what he had done. But his application for admission to the school was turned down because of the drawing. Even at this unformed stage, his work was too personal, too individual. His vision was his own and did not conform to the rigid standards of the school's tradition-bound board of experts.

Disappointed but not discouraged, Chagall did the only thing possible. He entered an easier school, one sponsored by the Imperial Society for the Protection of the Arts, a school meant for students unable to enter the Academy. There were three classes: one in which the students drew still lifes, pictures of inanimate objects such as a bowl of fruit or a vase of flowers; one in which they drew from plaster models; and one in which they drew from live models. Chagall's still lifes were a great success and attracted the attention of the director of the school. As a result, he was given a year's scholarship of fifteen rubles a month. With this money, he was able to eat a meal—almost every day—in a little restaurant.

But Chagall was not happy at the school. The teachers —with one exception—praised him, but he knew he was making no progress, a progress he could best measure himself. With no inspiration from the teachers, he felt his time at the school was wasted. Finally, after being reprimanded by Bobrovsky, the one teacher who never liked his work, he left the school forever.

Throughout the entire first part of his stay in Saint Petersburg, Chagall was plagued by the problem of the permit to remain in the capital. The one that had been arranged for by his father expired after a few months and could not

From *Dead Souls* by Gogol, Plate 37, *They Meet a Peasant* (Etching and Drypoint)
The Art Institute of Chicago

be renewed. One time, after returning from a visit to Vitebsk, he was even jailed for not having the permit. There seemed to be no solution to the problem. Because manual workers had little difficulty in obtaining permits, Chagall decided to learn a necessary skill. After much searching for a proper trade, he found a chance to become apprentice to a sign painter. He worked hard and in a way enjoyed it; he was pleased to see the signs he made gently rocking with the breeze above the shops; they reminded him of the signs he loved in Vitebsk, and perhaps of the sign outside Yehuda Pen's school, a sign that had played such an important part in his life. At the end of his apprenticeship came the final qualifying examination. If he could pass, he would be given a permit, but because he had trouble with the lettering, he failed.

Just when all seemed hopeless, the struggling young painter met a kindly, well-to-do lawyer named Goldberg. A patron of the arts, Goldberg recognized the young man's developing talent. When Chagall explained the problem of the permit to the lawyer, Goldberg had a solution. As a successful professional man, he was permitted to obtain residence permits for his servants. So it was that he pretended to hire Chagall as a footman and thus obtained for him the permit and allowed the painter to live in his home. Though young Chagall had to live in a small space under the stairs, the

From *My Life, House in Peskowatik* (Drypoint)
Collection, The Museum of Modern Art, New York

Goldberg family befriended him and occasionally invited him
to the family home in the country where he could paint.

Through Goldberg and his family, Chagall soon met
other art collectors. He would timidly go to their drawing

rooms and show them his work. Of these two were to be
of special importance in the life of the young painter. One
was Max Moisevitch Vinaver, an important member of the
Duma, or parliament. The other was Vinaver's brother-in-
law, Leopold Sev. Both these men were very active in trying
to bring about a rebirth of Jewish culture in Russia, and both
recognized the unique genius of Marc Chagall at an early
stage. Vinaver, who was almost like a father to Chagall, was
the first man to buy two of his paintings; and it was at the
home of Sev that Chagall first heard about Leon Bakst and
his classes at the Svanseva School.

The Svanseva School had been founded in Moscow in
1899 by a Russian painter who had lived in Paris. Because
of this influence, it was very different from all other Russian
schools of art. A few years after its founding, the school
was moved to Saint Petersburg and was given fresh life with
the appointment of Leon Bakst as a teacher. Bakst had lived
in Paris; he knew western Europe and was influenced by
its art and ideas. It was clear to Sev, who knew Bakst, that
this was the school at which the young Chagall could flourish and learn to grow as a painter. An appointment with
Bakst was arranged.

At one o'clock in the afternoon, Chagall, a letter of
recommendation from Sev in hand, timidly went for an inter-
view at the home of Bakst. Without the master's permission,

47

he could not enter the Svanseva School. Once again, as he had done for his first meeting with Pen in Vitebsk, he gathered together all of his drawings for approval. But he was even more nervous this time than he had been that day, a few years before, at Pen's. After all, Bakst had an international reputation; he was a famous, important man, and the young artist felt that what happened that afternoon would be a decisive factor in his career as a painter.

The door to Bakst's home on Sergiushkaja Street was opened by the master's maid, who told the anxious young painter that Bakst was still asleep but that he could wait for him. Chagall entered the silent room, and the maid left him alone. He nervously paced up and down. He looked at the walls—what he saw interested him far more than what he had seen at Pen's studio. There were all kinds of objects, paintings of Greek gods, a black velvet altar curtain from a synagogue, embroidered in silver. He noticed the time. It was one in the afternoon. Leon Bakst was still asleep! What a strange hour to be sleeping! But Bakst was different; he was a great man. His success in Paris was well known. During the great exhibition of Russian art which had taken place at the Grand Palais in Paris, Bakst had even designed a formal garden on the grounds of the Palais. A man like that was allowed to work and sleep when he wanted to.

After what seemed like several hours to the shy but

48

From *My Life,* Plate 18, *At the Easel* (Drypoint)
The Art Institute of Chicago

eager young Chagall, Leon Bakst appeared. He had red, curly hair and wasn't really frightening looking at all; his warm smile helped put the young man at ease. Chagall remembered that this world-famous man had started out much as he himself had. He had, in fact, come from a small town very near Vitebsk. Yet there was something different about him—it was western Europe—his clothing, his expression, his manner.

Smiling gently at the young painter before him, Bakst asked him what he wanted. Chagall, stammering, told him, and Bakst asked to see his sketches.

Once again, he stood by as a teacher examined his work. He felt more sure of himself than he had at Pen's, but Bakst was certain to be a more demanding critic.

Finally, Bakst spoke. "Ye . . . es . . . es . . . es! There's talent here; but you've been sp-oi-led, you're on the wrong track."

Spoiled, on the wrong track. It didn't matter. The master recognized his talent, he would allow him to be admitted to the school. A new world would be opened to him. Another step forward had been taken.

Chagall was at first frightened by the Svanseva School and the other pupils. Among the latter were the Countess Tolstoy, daughter of the great writer, author of *War and*

Peace, and Nijinsky, one of the greatest ballet dancers of all times, whose easel was next to Chagall's. And the school was so different from any other he had attended, from the dull-ness at Pen's and the stubborn rigidity at the school run by the Society for the Protection of the Arts.

There were classes in painting and in drawing, from models and from memory. All week the pupils would draw and paint, and on Fridays Bakst himself would come to see their work and comment on it. His approach was not at all like what Chagall was used to. He emphasized the use of color, the dramatic contrast and interplay of colors in his pupils' work. On these Fridays, he would criticize each stu-dent's paintings in front of the whole class, questioning the pupil's intentions, telling what he felt they were and in what way the pupil had succeeded or failed.

Chagall was particularly nervous about his teacher's comments, and he dreaded each Friday. The first Friday Bakst commented on Chagall's work, he was harsh and se-vere. The young man was upset. The following Friday was even worse. Bakst merely passed by his work without mak-ing any comment at all. Now, the young painter was dis-couraged. It was not that he felt he could not paint, but be-cause he was afraid he could not learn. Maybe he would always be a bad pupil, maybe he just had to go his own way. His doubts tormented him so that he left the school, without a word, and didn't return for three months.

During those three months, he worked harder than ever. Day and night he painted—experimenting with new forms and different colors. When he felt ready, he returned to the school. On the first Friday, he showed his latest study to Bakst. Happily, his teacher was pleased. The pupil had made progress on his own. Bakst thought the study was so good that he hung it on the wall of the studio.

BELLA

While living in Saint Petersburg, Chagall often visited Vitebsk—for weeks and even months at a time, especially during the summer. Through his friend Victor he met Thea Brachman, the daughter of a successful doctor. Thea spoke German, she had traveled, she played the piano, and she even wrote poetry. Through her, Chagall entered a new world, and his visits to her home were the high points of his stays in Vitebsk at the time.

The Brachmans lived on a small, quiet street near the railroad station. The street was half wood and half stone. The house itself was a small, one-story building, whose windows looked right out onto the busy sidewalk. Because of this, they were always shut, and heavy drapes kept out the light as well as the street noises. It was always cool and dark in the Brachman parlor, protected from the sounds of the carriages driving to the station and the *clip-clop* of the horses galloping along the broken cobblestones.

But the home was alive at all times. There was music— Thea and her brothers played the violin and piano, and at all hours the sounds of Mozart or Beethoven sonatas floated through the house. There were flowers, too, flowers every-where, gathered or bought by Thea's mother wherever she went. And birds—a room full of singing birds; and there was the old dog, Marquis. Most important, though, were the gay, laughing people. Marc loved to be with them, to discuss art and music and literature, new ideas.

He loved to be with Thea alone too and just relax in her world. Sometimes in the late afternoon, when Dr. Brach-man was out paying house calls, he would go to the house and stretch out on the long, black sofa in the doctor's con-sulting room, near the window. There he would look up at the ceiling and dream, or even fall asleep. During his visits to Vitebsk he lived in furnished rooms rented for him by his parents, and they were none too comfortable.

One such afternoon, as he was lying on the sofa—while Thea was preparing a dinner of fish, bread and butter—and hoping that the girl would soon come to sit near him, the doorbell rang. "It must be her father," Marc thought. "I'll have to get up and leave."

Self-Portrait, smiling (Etching and Drypoint)
The Art Institute of Chicago

As he listened, he realized it was not Thea's father—the voice was that of a young girl, who was talking on and on about a vacation, about foreign cities. He heard Thea pace up and down the room anxiously—she probably didn't want her friend to know he was there—but the girl just kept talking, going on about her holiday, the clothes she had bought and the people she had met.

Finally Marc couldn't stand it anymore. He had to see who it was. Quietly, he got up from the sofa and opened up the door that led to the living room. The girl's back was to him, and she was still talking. "Thea, you know I laughed so much. What a pity you weren't there. . . ."

Marc stood there silently. There was something about the way that girl was standing, her voice, her manner. Slowly he approached the two girls; with embarrassment, he laughed.

The girl turned around, startled. A strange boy in Thea's home! He looked like he had been sleeping there. So peculiar looking, so different from the other boys she had known. That funny hair, with all those curls, forming little rings, hanging over his forehead. The almond-shaped eyes, so full of life. Yes, he was beautiful in a way, but there was something wild about him. No wonder Thea didn't want her to know he was there.

Marc continued to laugh nervously. The girl was frightened; she didn't know what to do, what to think, what to say. Her best friend Thea just stood there, not even introducing them. The three young people stood silently in the middle of the room. Then, all at once, Marc approached the young girl, still not saying a word. Finally, the young girl spoke. "Thea, I have to go home," she stammered.

Marc looked at her. "Why, where are you rushing to? You have such a pretty voice. I heard you laughing."

Desperately, the girl turned to Thea, who suddenly spoke. "Bella, this is the artist; you know, I told you about him."

But it was too late. While Thea was trying to explain, the young girl grabbed her hat and cape and ran out of the door.

Bella ran towards the river bank, bewildered. She didn't know what had come over her. This Marc Chagall was not the first artist she had met—among others, she knew Victor Mekler well. The Rosenfelds, her parents, were one of the richest, most cultivated families in Vitebsk. Through her travels with her mother to Berlin, to Vienna, to Marienbad where they spent their summers, she had met all kinds of people—artists, writers, and musicians, as well as worldly businessmen. But, she thought, there was something different about this boy. He seemed to her like a twinkling star; that was it. He was broad and strong, and he was handsome, but he seemed to have no feet, seemed somehow to be floating. Though he had kept laughing, she was sure that was because he was shy. She did remember Thea talking about him, how poor he was and how hard he worked. Thea obviously knew him well, but why had she never introduced him to her before? She had made him sound so dedicated and she always said his paintings were so profound. She remembered too how Thea had said it was important to help these young, struggling artists.

Bewildered, confused, Bella reached the bridge over the Dvina. She was halfway home and, exhausted, she stopped to rest. The river was swollen, and its waters lapped against the muddy banks. An icy wind blew across her face as she looked over the river. There was a little boat in the distance —was it in the sky or in the water? She wanted to stretch out on the cold waves and hold a piece of cloud in her hands. How she loved the sky and the water!

But she was thinking about that boy again. She could almost feel his presence. How would he describe what she felt and saw?

There was something at her feet, brushing against her. Startled, she looked down. It was Thea's dog, Marquis, licking her with his warm tongue. As she turned around, she saw Thea and Marc. He was still laughing and even Thea was smiling now. How long had they been standing behind her at the bridge? And why were they laughing at her? Was it because they knew what she was thinking? For a moment, Bella was angry. She had had the good sense to leave them alone in the house, now why couldn't they leave her alone on the bridge? She wanted to run away again, but now she was surrounded—Marc on one side and Thea on the other. And Thea seemed sad . . . what could it be?

The young man interrupted her thoughts. "Come, let's walk together."

They began to walk on, and Bella felt a strange enchantment as he spoke. "Look, look here. There, in the corner, a light cloud is rising. Look at the color—a pearl gray. See? Now it's turned to a gray-black, like steel. Watch how it turns around."

With that Marc too turned around and around. Bella looked at him, suddenly happy as she had never been before. She and this strange young painter were seeing things in the same way. It was marvelous. But Thea, poor Thea, seemed sadder than ever. Had she in some way taken this boy away from Thea? Is that what Thea, her dearest friend, thought? No! She didn't ask them to follow her to the bridge. Suddenly angry, she turned toward the two of them:

"I have to go home. My mother is waiting for me."

"Then we'll go along with you," the boy said, smiling.

"No, no . . . I have to run. It's late, and my mother is waiting for me."

Without another word, she quickly ran home; once there, she went to her room, fell to the window ledge, and buried herself in her beloved books. But she knew then that something had happened, something that would change her life.

As Bella ran breathlessly across the bridge, Marc too knew that his life was changed. He didn't want to be with Thea any longer; he wanted to be with this girl forever. Her pale face, her large, round black eyes—she was the most beautiful girl he had ever seen. He felt he had always known her, that she had always known him.

The following day, Bella returned to the bridge. It was from the bridge and only from the bridge that she could see the sky, otherwise hidden by the church domes and rooftops of the town. And now the bridge had a special meaning for her. As she leaned over, looking first at the river and then at the sky, she imagined a crowd behind her. Suddenly, a hat was over her head.

"Good evening. Don't be afraid. It's me."

It was Marc Chagall. What was he doing there? Did he think she had come there to look for him? She was frightened.

"What are you afraid of?" he asked. "Are you taking a walk? So am I. Let's walk together."

Bella felt warm and reassured. In some way, he seemed

60

From *Dead Souls* by Gogol, *Frontispiece* (Drypoint)
The Art Institute of Chicago

part of her family. He wasn't laughing any more, either. His hand, which was warm and strong, reached out for hers. "Come on, we'll go down to the river bank and walk there. It's very pretty. Don't be afraid; I know the bank. I live there."

Marc led her down the steps from the bridge to the river. The bridge hung over them, and Marc did seem at home there, under it and along the river.

"Let's sit down over there," he suggested, pointing to some birch logs not far away.

Silently, they walked along the Dvina. They were happy; there was a bond between them. "What," thought Bella, "would Mother think if she knew I was walking along the dark banks of the river . . . and not with my girl friends, but with a strange boy?" She could almost hear her mother's voice scolding her and feel her slapping her face!

Marc and Bella continued to see each other. They enjoyed one another's company, they enjoyed wandering through the town and along the river. But they were both shy, and their meetings were in secret. Little by little, they began to share their thoughts and feelings. Even Bella, who was sometimes called the Queen of Silence, found she could speak freely and happily to Marc. But one day the secret was out.

It was Sabbath eve, and Bella was spending it quietly at home with her family. Somewhat bored and restless, she asked her brother Mendel to go for a walk with her.

"Are you crazy?" asked Mendel. "No one goes walking after supper on Friday. And it's so late."

But Bella knew how to convince her brother. "Come on, we'll go and have a glass of seltzer."

That did it, for Mendel, like all the boys of Vitebsk, was always ready for a glass of seltzer.

The brother and sister set out for Budrovitch's seltzer shop, down by the railroad station; they knew it was open late, even on Friday night. All was still as they walked up one street and down another; lights were out; the town was asleep. They reached the river, and Bella breathed in the fresh, clean air and looked at the shimmering stars. They jumped about so that she was sure they wanted to leap down from the sky right onto the earth.

They crossed the street into the center of the town. The sky was now hidden; starlight no longer illuminated the town. Not only were the stores closed, but their signs were no longer visible. But it didn't matter; Bella knew the way, past the drygoods store, with its sleeping wooden models, past the bookstore, its walls covered with the books among which she loved to wander; and past the photographer's shop, filled with gold frames around empty spaces.

From *My Life,* Plate 15, *Lovers on the Bench* (Etching)
The Art Institute of Chicago

As they came closer to the station, rays of light fell at
their feet, light from the seltzer shop. People were milling
around the door. In the shop itself, there was excitement as
the fizzling seltzer was spurted into the glasses. To Bella, it
sounded like someone blowing his nose. Seltzer gushed out as
from a spring and whistled in the glasses. She and Mendel

drank, the bubbles tickling their nostrils and biting their throats.

Their drinks finished, they happily left the shop. They were stopped by a voice. "It's you. . . . What are you doing here? Why do you go walking so late at night?"

It was Marc, of course. How had he found her? Bella turned nervously towards her brother.

"Well," said Mendel. "Who is this?" He pointed suspiciously at Marc.

Bella was horrified. The scandal was out in the open. From the way the strange boy had approached her, from the familiar way he spoke to her, it was obvious that he knew Bella well. It was awful; what could Mendel be thinking? He knew all of Bella's friends—and they were all girls. Why, she didn't even have much to do with the brothers of her girl friends. She was too shy. But, here was this strange boy; and he was strange, the way he was dressed. . . .

Mendel stared at Marc. No, he had never seen him before—maybe he wasn't even from Vitebsk. With such long and curly hair, he had to be—a painter! His sister Bella, the daughter of one of the best families in Vitebsk, going around with a painter. . . . He looked angrily at her. His little sister, a child, a toy for Mendel and his brothers to play with. They adored their little sister. Now, suddenly, she had grown up before his eyes; she was almost a woman, and no different from the others. Worse. This young man who must be a painter looked like an animal that had escaped from the forest.

Bella stood awkwardly between Marc and Mendel. She wanted Marc to say something, to prove to her older brother that he was normal and sensible, in spite of his wild hair. But Mendel moved away from them, and Marc remained silent. Bella was frightened. Mendel would, she feared, run home with the news: "Bella has a boy friend." He would tell the news to everyone and keep the worst part for the end: the boy friend was a painter. What could she ever tell her mother? Her mother would never believe that he was a friend of Thea's. It was too terrible; to give one more worry to her mother who had more than enough worries with her brothers.

And what was the matter with Marc? Why did he have to come out at this time of night, and then show up at the seltzer shop? And then why did he stand there without saying a word to Mendel? Just staring with those warm, flashing eyes that seemed to see more than the eyes of the other young men of Vitebsk.

Without warning, Marc turned to her. "Your throat is yellow; your skin is yellow."

Bella jumped back. This was too much. She couldn't believe her ears. Talking about her throat and skin like that, in the middle of the street, in front of her brother, too. Why, he hadn't ever seen her throat, and he knew nothing about the color of her skin. He was either drunk or crazy. Always talking about things in terms of color; his eyes must be constantly filled with color.

Bella began to cry with shame. She felt her throat, her dress, her high collar. That was it! The dress she was wearing had yellow embroidery at the neck. She shouted out: "It's just trimming, yellow trimming, don't you see that? And you call yourself a painter!" How she wished she could tear off the embroidery and throw it in his face to show him which was yellow, the trimming or her skin.

Angry and hurt, she dragged her stunned brother by the arm. "Come on, Mendel. Come home."

And a puzzled Marc was left behind, standing in the middle of the street.

Before long, it didn't matter who knew about their friendship or what they said about it. Bella and Marc understood each other and loved each other. They would often meet at the cafe above her father's main jewelry shop (he owned three of them), and Bella would come to visit her painter wherever he worked or lived. Whenever he came to Vitebsk from Saint Petersburg, it was to Bella that he came first. She inspired him and helped him in his work, criticizing it gently and sensitively, always encouraging him.

One day, it became clear to Marc that Bella would become his wife. When he proposed that they become engaged, she joyously accepted. Of course, there was opposition. Bella Rosenfeld was from one of the wealthiest Jewish families of Vitebsk. Her family's jewelry and watch shops were the finest in town. They lived in a beautiful home and had a cook. Bella, their pride and joy, was not only rich; she was also beautiful and brilliant. When she graduated from high school, she was given a gold medal as one of the four best graduates in all of Russia. At the time she met Marc, she had been studying at one of the finest girls' schools in Moscow. Was it right that such an outstanding girl should love and even talk about marrying the son of such a poor family? And, even worse, a painter?

None of this mattered. Bella Rosenfeld and Marc Chagall belonged together.

TO A NEW LIFE

While in Vitebsk, Chagall painted as much as he did when studying in Saint Petersburg. Bella was a constant source of inspiration for him, and in 1909, soon after meeting her, he painted the first of many portraits of his future wife. It was called *Portrait of My Fiancée in Black Gloves*.

It is a surprising picture for a romantic young man of twenty-two, in love for the first time—and with the subject of this portrait. For Bella stands rather stiffly, hands on her hips, her face unsmiling. She is dressed in a white dress, with a ruffled collar. The whiteness of her dress contrasts with the black background, the blue beret, and the black gloves she wears. There is an almost classic beauty about this painting and, it seems at first, a coldness. But as we examine it, we see what Chagall must have felt: an idealized love for a strong, determined, and very beautiful woman, a spiritual being.

This painting, probably the most famous he was ever to do of Bella, shows a new, serious phase in the artist's work that began after his return to Vitebsk from Saint Petersburg. The gay charming scenes of his town that he had painted in the past were somehow more somber; there is a sadness about them that, perhaps, denotes a new maturity.

Chagall was making so much progress with his painting that by spring of 1910 he began to feel as closed in by Saint Petersburg as he had by Vitebsk a few years before. He had learned all he could learn there. The artistic climate of the Russian capital was not ready for the modern work that appealed to Chagall. It was at that time, too, that Leon Bakst decided to leave Saint Petersburg for Paris, to work as scene designer for the great impresario Sergei Diaghilev, who had founded the Russian Ballet in Paris in 1909 and was having great success there. Paris! That's where Chagall wanted to be, where he had to go!

He approached Bakst and begged him to take him with him, to use him as an assistant scene designer. Bakst agreed on the condition that the young man learn to paint scenery; he even gave him money to learn. Chagall did his best, working hard to earn his way as Bakst's assistant. At the end of his lessons, he was given a test: he was to do sketches for a ballet called *Narcissus*. Once again, his originality cost him an opportunity. From his sketches it was obvious that he would be unable to be a simple assistant to Bakst, to follow the master's orders. The older man's conventional approach was not Chagall's. Not only did Bakst refuse to take the young painter with him; he discouraged him altogether from going, warning him that he might starve in the French capital.

But Marc Chagall's mind was made up; he had to go to Paris, just as he had had to leave Vitebsk for Saint Petersburg. The move took great courage; once again, life would be difficult. He knew that he was taking a great chance, that he might well starve as Bakst had suggested. The change would be enormous—a new city, a new climate, new people, a new language. But he knew enough about Paris to realize that only there could he find the true language he was seeking—the language of art.

Though this time there was no problem of a permit, the financial problem remained. More than thirty thousand painters had come to Paris; many went hungry. Fortunately, Max Vinaver came to his rescue. He had faith in the young painter, and he too knew that he could best develop in Paris, so he granted him a monthly allowance for his stay there.

Chagall spent the early part of the summer of 1910 with Bella and his family in Vitebsk. It was a happy time during which his love for Bella grew. He hated to leave her, and he was sad and afraid to leave his home country, but he knew

71

that he was now grown up. He had to go ahead, to go out into the world and face it. His world was to be found in Paris.

In August, he gathered together all his possessions, his oils, his drawings, and his gouaches—paintings done with an opaque watercolor prepared with gum. He boarded the train, and after four long days he arrived in Paris.

Paris through the Window (1913)
The Solomon R. Guggenheim Museum Collection

Portrait of my Fiancée in Black Gloves
Kunstmuseum, Basel, Switzerland
Colorphoto Hinz, Basel

I and my Village (ca. 1911)
Collection, Philadelphia Museum of Art

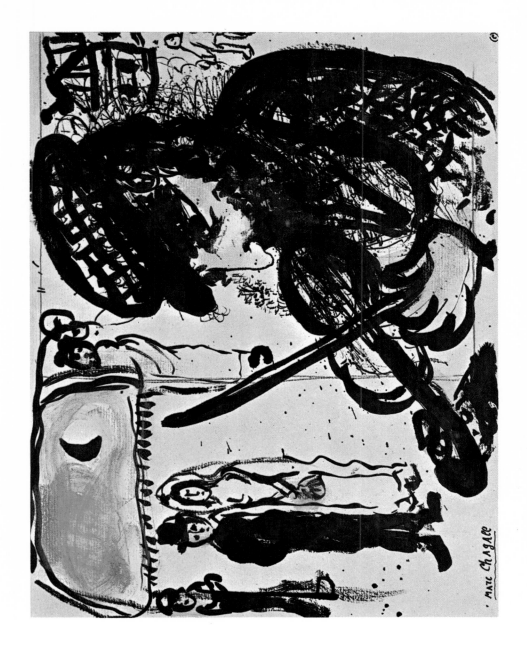

The Wedding (1911)   Mr. and Mrs. Victor Babin, Shaker Heights, Ohio

PARIS

When Marc Chagall got off that train in the summer of 1910, he was entering the most exciting city in the world. He was to remain there for four years.

During this period, the capital of France was also the artistic and cultural capital of the world. It seemed that everything was happening there—new ideas, new creations, all bubbling with excitement. Artists from all over the world had gathered there: from Italy, Amedeo Modigliani and Giorgio de Chirico; from Spain, Pablo Picasso and Juan Gris; from Roumania, Jules Pascin; and from Lithuania, Chaim Soutine; from Russia, the great composer Igor Stravinsky and the sculptor Alexander Archipenko. Indeed, Russian culture was contributing heavily to the intellectual life of Paris. There was the great season of ballet presented by Diaghilev. To the acclaim of all Paris, they danced

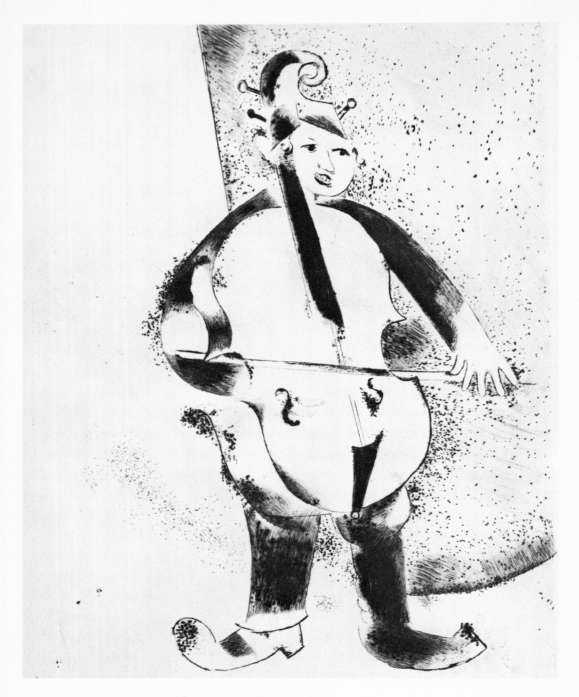

The Musician (Drypoint)
The Solomon R. Guggenheim Museum

Scheherazade, choreographed by Fokine, with music by Rimsky-Korsakov; *The Firebird*, with Stravinsky's music; *Giselle, Carnaval, Les Sylphides*. Bakst had designed many of the sets and costumes, and Nijinsky, the dancer whose easel had been next to Chagall's at the Svanseva School, was the star of the company, a marvelous performer who was to startle the world with his remarkable performance in the ballet *Spectre of the Rose,* at the end of which he seemed to fly through the window. During this period too, Stravinsky changed the course of ballet music with his brilliant score for *Petrushka,* shortly after which Paris was to hear the premiere of the then startling and now familiar *The Rites of Spring*. Russia was represented as well in the theater—there were dramatizations of two works by Feodor Dostoevski, and a full season by the famous Moscow Art Theatre.

The year 1913 was to be an important one for French literature, too. Marcel Proust's *Swann's Way* was published then as was Guillaume Apollinaire's *Alcools* and some works of Colette.

It was to this exciting world that the flashing-eyed, curly-haired young painter came in 1910. French art and culture were being enriched by fresh currents from all over the world; they would soon be further enriched by the brilliant new sense of color, the humor, the poetry, and unashamed warmth of Marc Chagall's art.

83

But first it was Paris, the enchanting city of light and color which gave of itself to Chagall, and which nourished the painter from Vitebsk. As was to be expected, the newness of it frightened Chagall when he arrived. Only the great distance, the four days' journey, that separated him from his home prevented him from turning right back. The traffic, the crowds, the sheer brilliance of the magical city were almost too much for him. After the drabness of his home, he felt almost blinded at first. Soon, however, it was to become an overwhelming feast for his eyes, his mind, his soul.

Victor Mekler, his old friend from Vitebsk, had come to Paris before him and was at the station when he arrived. Chagall was happy to see a familiar face and gratefully accepted Victor's invitation to share his home for the first few days. It did make things easier those first days, but it was clear that the two friends had grown apart. Victor could no longer understand Chagall's art, and the latter was unable to appreciate his old friend's mediocre paintings that seemed to him little more than photographic representations. In a few days, Chagall was offered two rooms that belonged to another Russian painter who was to be away from Paris for a while, and it was there that he settled.

Once in his new quarters, Chagall began to visit the

many museums and galleries that Paris had to offer. He was exhilarated, thrilled beyond his greatest hopes. He felt most at home in the Louvre, the great museum along the Seine. As he studied the works of the great masters there—Rembrandt, Delacroix, Chardin, Courbet, Uccello and others—he felt he was visiting old friends. They had expressed themselves as he wanted to, and he spent endless hours looking at their works in astonished joy. Before their works, he felt humble, but he also gained strength and courage. How right he had been to come to Paris!

He spent hours too in the smaller galleries, studying the works of contemporary French painters. There were the marvelous landscapes, still lifes and portraits of Paul Cézanne, the master who had died only a few years before; the violent, vibrant paintings of Vincent Van Gogh; the works of Paul Gauguin, the brilliant colorist who had lived much of his life in the South Pacific. Paintings by Henri Matisse, Auguste Renoir . . . Shortly after his arrival, too, he visited the exhibition called the Salon des Independants, where works by Pierre Bonnard, Albert Gleizes, and Matisse were hung. His joy and excitement were almost unbearable; each day was adventure, almost a rebirth. He has since written that he was indeed born again in Paris, that it was his second Vitebsk.

Stimulated by his new environment, he began to work at once. He painted scenes remembered from Vitebsk, and

Promenade (Etching)
The Art Institute of Chicago

he painted scenes of Paris. The money from Vinaver was helpful, but it was not enough, and often he lacked the means to buy canvas. However, nothing could stop him; if he had no money for new canvases, he would buy old paintings— which were cheaper—and paint them over. More than ever, he had to paint.

One of his best-known and most important works from this period in Paris was *I and My Village,* which was painted in 1911. It is a memory, a fable of Vitebsk, a symbol of the artist's relationship with his own town. It is Chagall's love for Vitebsk seen with the new vision and techniques acquired in Paris. At first, the painting seems complicated. It is made up of interweaving circles and triangles. Dominating one side is the smiling green face of a peasant. In his hand (there is a red-jeweled ring on his finger) he holds a sprig of flowers; this dominates the lower portion of the picture. The flowers reach almost to the mouth of a cow's head, which dominates the other side of the picture. In the cow's head we see a girl milking a cow. On the top of the canvas, a miniature town. There is a row of houses—two of them upside down—and a church with the priest's face framed in it. Just below the town is a farmer with a scythe and next to him an upside-down woman.

The more we examine the painting, the more we discover in it. It isn't logical, of course, but art is not logic. It is, on the other hand, a brilliant evocation of a town, its people and its way of life. The composition, the balance, the colors all add to make this an experience for those who look at the painting. It is possible to give it a concrete interpretation. Indeed, one art critic feels that the green-faced man thinks of his sweetheart milking a cow as he looks at the cow's head, which explains the milkmaid in the cow's head. But on this point, Chagall himself has said: "In my painting *I and My Village,* I painted a small cow and a milkmaid in the head of a large cow because I needed that kind of shape in that place for my composition." Whatever the reason, and whatever the interpretation, this and other paintings of the period marked an evolution in Chagall's work.

Though he attended two art schools, they were of little importance to him. He learned his lessons from the city itself, not only from its art but also from its people and places, the faces of the workmen and waiters, the many-shaded buildings, all illuminated by the life-giving light of Paris. That light shone through his work and deepened his colors. He was finding the way in Paris.

The rooms he had rented from the Russian artist were in Montparnasse, the center of the city's artistic life at that time. It was there that he was to meet and know the important young painters who had come to the capital—the French ones as well as the foreigners who had come as he had, to seek their artistic identity.

From *My Life,* Plate 11, *House in Vitebsk* (Drypoint)
The Art Institute of Chicago

Montparnasse throbbed with life, night and day. At one important cross section were two famous cafes: the Cafe du Dome, the meeting place of the Germans and Americans who came there to discuss the latest trends in French painting; and across the street, the Rotonde, at first the home for all Russian, Polish, and eastern European painters, and later the most important cafe for all of Paris's young artists. Artists would gather there, to drink their coffee and talk; at any time of day or night one could find Picasso, or maybe

Utrillo and his mother, Suzanne Valadon, also a painter; perhaps there would be Andre Derain or Maurice Vlaminck or Fernand Léger. Modigliani, too, the moody Italian painter, came there as did Apollinaire, the poet and critic who was to play an important part in Chagall's life. There were heated discussions on art, politics, life itself and its meaning.

Near the cafes themselves, the shop windows were filled with artists' materials—canvases, brushes, and tubes of paint. And on Mondays there was what amounted to a market for human models, bizarre looking men and women, all hoping to be chosen as subject matter for one painter or another. And every day there was Hazard, the clever shopkeeper who learned to cater to the international gathering by selling grapefruits to the Americans, salmon eggs to the Russians, sauerkraut to the Germans, and paprika-flavored sausages to the Hungarians.

In those years between 1910 and 1914, foreigners were arriving in greater and greater numbers—young men willing to live in dark, dingy, cramped quarters on near-starvation diets, in order to breathe the air and spirit of Paris. Marc Chagall was no different from the rest. He would sit alone at the Dome, chewing on a piece of bread given him by a sympathetic baker and sipping his coffee—how often this would be his only food for the day! But it didn't matter. He had Paris.

The young artists of Montparnasse worked hard, but they also played hard. Many a night was spent at wild parties, singing and drinking until dawn. Chagall avoided all of this; he was too serious and dedicated to let anything take him from his work. Nonetheless, he did get to know the important artists and writers of the time. He was especially pleased at the results of his visit to the Russian Ballet. He went there, somewhat nervously, to see his old classmate Nijinsky and to show Leon Bakst that, in spite of his advice, he had had the courage to come to Paris.

"So you came after all," was the way his old teacher greeted him. As they parted backstage at the ballet, Bakst promised to come by Chagall's studio to see the work he had been doing. Much to Chagall's surprise, Bakst did come. Slowly and carefully, he studied the paintings: the boy he had taught had really grown up. "Now," he told his former pupil, "your colors sing."

Chagall's colors did sing, and he worked harder and harder, at the same time entering into the artistic life, learning from new people and their new ideas as he did from the museums, galleries, streets, and shop windows of Paris. He especially enjoyed his visits to the home of Robert and Sonia Delaunay, two well-known painters, where he would discuss the newest schools of painting. The Delaunays were especially influenced by futurism which called for a new approach to

From *Dead Souls* by Gogol, Plate 19 (Etching and Drypoint)
The Art Institute of Chicago

art through the portrayal of dynamic movement and force. In addition, Friday evenings became important for Chagall, for it was then that he would go to the home of Canudo, the editor of an avant-garde magazine called *Montjoie,* where he would have a chance to meet and talk to many other leading artists of Paris, some of them men whose work he had earlier admired in the city's galleries.

Chagall's horizons expanded even further when he gave up the rooms he had lived in since the first days after his arrival and moved into a building that has since become a legend. Its name was La Ruche, or the beehive, and it was so called because of its twelve-sided shape. La Ruche had been the dream of a minor painter and sculptor named Alfred Boucher who had always wanted to establish inexpensive lodgings and studios for struggling artists. For this purpose, he had bought—at a very low price—this twelve-sided structure that had originally been built for and used as an exhibit hall during the great Universal Exposition in Paris in 1900. It was located in an area which combined the features of city and country, very close to the largest slaughterhouses of Paris. In addition to this central building, Boucher bought others from the Exposition and placed them around La Ruche itself. When Chagall moved there, the whole complex was made up of 140 studios; he himself lived in the main building where there were twenty-four. There were twelve ground-floor studios for sculptors and another twelve on the second floor for painters. Above the door of each room was a small balcony and on it a bed. On one side of the room, a stove, and a third side was blank. It was that side that the artist would use for his easel and paints.

Though they were all young and relatively unknown at the time, some of this century's greatest artists lived in, or for a while stayed in, La Ruche. Modigliani had a studio next to Chagall's. The tempestuous, tormented Lithuanian Soutine often spent the night at La Ruche, and among its other inhabitants were Léger, Henri Laurens, Archipenko, and Jacques Lipschitz, all of whom grew to be artists of great importance.

Chagall worked feverishly, often through the night. He painted his dreams and his memories to the accompaniment of cries from the nearby slaughterhouses—how they must have reminded him of the sounds he had heard at his grandfather's butcher shop back in Russia! Throughout the night, too, came the sounds from the other studios—songs, guitar music, loud and often angry debates. Through it all the young man from Vitebsk painted. When even old canvases were unavailable, he would paint on tablecloths, on sheets, even sometimes on nightshirts. Nothing could keep him from his work, and he would spend entire nights alone in his studio, by the light of a kerosene lamp.

The room itself was a picture of total confusion. Pictures everywhere, eggshells, empty soup cans. On the shelves, reproductions of El Greco and Cézanne next to the remains of a herring and stale crusts of bread. Chagall was interested in only one thing: his work. It was his passion; neatness, parties, and good clothing only distracted him from this work.

While the agitated, tumultuous artistic life went on about him, he stayed away from crowds. When he wasn't

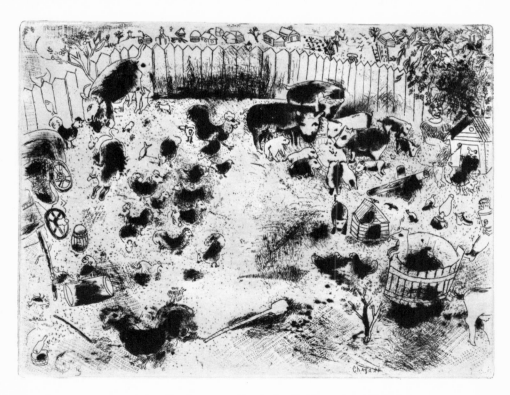

From *Dead Souls* by Gogol, *The Barnyard* (Etching)
Collection, The Museum of Modern Art, New York, Larry Aldrich Fund

painting or visiting museums and galleries, he wandered through the city's fascinating streets, taking in the colors and shapes, inspired by their beauty. He listened to music and he read, always curious and always interested. Unlike so many other struggling painters, he accepted no random charity; he paid for what he bought, and he bought only what he could afford. His friends and neighbors considered him "different." To them, he was a poet, a strange poet, full of original and often startling ideas, and these ideas, his treatment of them, and his wild use of color, were apart from the main current of French culture. La Ruche was a world apart from all commercial concerns, but Chagall, in a way, lived away from the world of La Ruche as well. He painted his memories and he painted Vitebsk while in his Parisian studio; only a few of his paintings were themselves set in Paris, and these few emphasized the marvelous symbol of the city, the Eiffel Tower. But, though he might not have painted the city itself, Paris and its light and warmth and colors were present throughout his brilliant work.

Two of Chagall's most important friendships during these four years in Paris were with two of France's leading poets, Guillaume Apollinaire and Blaise Cendrars. Poetry, lyric poetry, at the time was especially close to Chagall. He avidly read the works of the modern poets and found much connection between his works and their words. And they

found, in turn, reflections of their words in his lyrical painting. Chagall did not paint objects and scenes as a camera
would see them. He retained his own vision and, true to it,
his paintings were not what would be considered "logical."
His painting was truly close in spirit to poetry. Another great
painter, Georges Braque, put it well: "Every poet has a right
to say that a swallow soaring up to the sky is a dagger," he
wrote. "Should we painters not also have the right to paint
a dagger instead of the swallow?"

The poet closest to Chagall was Blaise Cendrars, a great
lyrical innovator. He had just returned from a trip around
the world when he met Chagall. A warm, passionate man, he
visited Chagall's studio and immediately sensed the genius of
the young painter's art; he felt close to it, and the two men
would spend hours together in the studio. Cendrars would
stare out the window and read his poetry aloud to an ap-
preciative Chagall. Together they would examine Chagall's
paintings, laughing together, share their ideas and thoughts.
Chagall found his painting in Cendrars' poetry, and the
latter found his poetry in his friend's painting.

Chagall's relationship with Apollinaire was a different,
less intimate matter, but equally important. Apollinaire was
one of the leading literary and artistic figures of the period.
A poet of great strength and lyricism, he was also an important art critic and one of the guiding spirits of the move-

ment known as cubism which developed in France in 1907 and was led, in the field of visual art, by Picasso and Braque. It might best be defined as attempts by painters to reduce objects, figures, and even landscapes to their basic geometric forms. Though influenced by cubism as any artist is influenced by all that surrounds him—its influence is perhaps most felt in *I and My Village,* which was painted during this period—Chagall was not at all dominated by it. He could not then, nor could he ever, become part of a group and blindly follow its rules. Because of this, because he was not a follower of cubism, he somewhat warily approached Apollinaire, the man so dedicated to the movement.

The two men first met at the poet's apartment near Montparnasse. It was an odd home, at the top of a small building, reached by such a narrow staircase that it seemed like a ladder. The apartment itself was small and crowded with heavy furniture. Shelves and tables were covered with every kind of object, and even the narrow hallway had shelves, these filled with yellowing paperback books. The ceiling was low, and on the walls hung paintings by the leading cubist painters—Picasso, Derain, Chirico, among others. Confusion was total, much as it was in Chagall's own home, and through it all wandered Apollinaire's faithful cat.

But Chagall liked it all, and when the poet emerged from his corner bedroom, he knew that he would like Apollinaire too. There was a broad smile on his face and in his gentle eyes. The two men became friends, and Chagall was often a visitor to the poet's garret.

Even as their friendship developed, Chagall found it difficult to ask this standard bearer of cubism to La Ruche to see his paintings. One day, however, he summoned up the courage. The two men were having lunch; Chagall, as always, was astounded by Apollinaire's great appetite. Maybe, he thought, it takes so much food to feed such an enormous talent. During the meal, all the great and near greats stopped by to pay their respects to their leader. It was impressive and stimulating, as always, to be with Apollinaire. Once the meal was finished, Chagall made up his mind—he invited the poet to La Ruche. The leader of cubism accepted the invitation with pleasure. He knew Chagall was no follower of his movement, but it didn't matter.

As they walked up the narrow staircase at La Ruche, Chagall had misgivings. He was sure Apollinaire would never approve of his work. As for the poet, as he entered the small studio, he was more afraid that the fragile old wood building would collapse under his weight.

The two men entered the room, and Apollinaire looked around him, at the flying cows, the upside-down figures, the vivid colors. He sat down. Smiling and blushing, he whispered one word: "Supernatural." Though his own work was not close to Chagall's, he too felt akin to the paintings of the young man from Vitebsk. More than that, he was genuinely enthusiastic about the happy and sad lyricism, and the wonderful fantasy in the paintings. When he left the studio at La Ruche, he wrote a poem to Chagall, in which he speaks of his "visit to the round house where a salt herring swims," and in which he describes Chagall as having hair "like the trolley cable across Europe arrayed in little, many colored fires." Apollinaire, too, was able to understand and enter into the personal world of Marc Chagall.

BERLIN, AND RECOGNITION

In March, 1913, Apollinaire introduced Chagall to Herwarth Walden, a German art patron and dealer. A little owlish man, with hair flowing to his shoulders and a jerking, hoplike walk, Walden had both a passion for and an excellent taste in art. In Berlin he had founded an influential magazine called *Der Sturm,* or *The Storm,* as well as an art gallery of that name. Much of his spare time was spent traveling through Europe in search of exciting new artists.

Walden met Chagall at Apollinaire's home. He was quite impressed by the curious young Russian with the bright eyes and curly hair. When Apollinaire suggested to Walden that he put on an exhibit of Chagall's work at his Berlin gallery, Walden agreed to go to La Ruche and see his work. He did so the following day and immediately offered to ex-

Drawing by Chagall from *Le Dur Desir de Durer*
(by Paul Eluard; Arnold-Bordas, Paris)

hibit the young painter's work in the "First German Autumn Salon," which was modeled after the famous annual exhibits in Paris. It was to be held in Walden's gallery. Chagall was overjoyed. Perhaps his big chance had come.

His recognition in Paris had been limited. During his stay there, his paintings had been displayed three times in the Salon des Independants and once in the Autumn Salon, but they were hardly noticed. Some of his work was also shown in Amsterdam and in an exhibition of French painters in Moscow, but he had not become known and did not sell any paintings. It was so bad that one day when a dealer, Malpel, who was later to offer Chagall a small monthly subsidy, spoke of buying one of Chagall's paintings at the Salon *if* no one else bought it, Chagall said, "Why wait?"

He just wasn't selling. One gallery kindly allowed him to leave thirty of his gouaches there; they remained unsold for several months. Though the young painter was not discouraged, for nothing could stop his art any more, he was bound to be disappointed at his lack of recognition in Paris. He had worked hard and grown immeasurably as a painter, but his circle of admirers was a small one, for his paintings were too personal, too far from the main currents, unable to fit into any of the neat classifications he so deplored.

In May, 1914, he left Paris for Berlin to attend his first one-man show, which was being organized by Walden.

103

Through an exhibition of his work alone, he had to be recognized and noticed. After Berlin, he was planning to return briefly to Vitebsk—to attend his sister's wedding and to see his beloved Bella, with whom he had continued to correspond—before returning to Paris. He left his paintings behind, and the door to his studio at La Ruche open, never guessing that it would be almost nine years before he could return to the city in which he had become Marc Chagall, a painter and a man.

Berlin was humming with activity when Chagall arrived there. The German Expressionist movement—in which painters expressed their inner feelings rather than their impressions of the external—was dominant, with its brilliant leaders such as Paul Klee, Wassily Kandinsky, Franz Marc, and Auguste Macke. Chagall's work was a great success with this group, but personal contact was limited because of the Russian's inability to speak German.

Chagall's exhibition opened in early June at Der Sturm gallery on Potsdammerstrasse; shown were forty oil paintings and 160 gouaches, watercolors and drawings. The gallery was so crowded that even the tables and a part of the floor were covered with drawings. It was a huge success, and Chagall could well have stayed on to enjoy his new fame. But, anxious to see his Bella, he boarded the train for Russia on June 15, 1914. Before he left, he sent a postcard to his friend Robert Delaunay in Paris which read:

"It is warm, it is raining, sauerkraut. German girls are quite extraordinarily not pretty. I am leaving today: Vitebsk. Pokrovskaja."

RETURN TO VITEBSK

Marc Chagall returned to Vitebsk a changed man. Of course, he had matured in four years, but more than the mere passing of time, it was the light of Paris and the real discovery of his art that had changed him.

Vitebsk itself had not changed, unfortunately, but it seemed quite different to Chagall from when he had last seen it. Four years before, he had felt vaguely imprisoned there, but now—after having lived in Paris and come in contact with western art—he found his native town strange, boring, and unhappy. He missed the gaiety and excitement of Paris, and its people. Here in Vitebsk, he seemed to be surrounded by uncles and aunts, all of them telling him how big he had grown. He was determined to make good use of his time there—a short time, he expected—and then return

From *My Life,* Plate 5, *Pokrova Street* (Drypoint)
The Art Institute of Chicago

107

to Paris as soon as possible. At that point he could not have guessed that history—in the form of the Russian Revolution and World War I—would change his plans.

Never able to be unactive, Chagall the painter did something that turned out to be of great value. With his newly developed sense of color and techniques, he started to paint a series of pictures which could be called documents of Vitebsk. It was, he must have sensed, the beginning of the end of an era, an end of the town as he had known it in his childhood, an end of a way of life. For this reason, he furiously painted everything, everyone in sight—his parents, his brother, his sisters, the houses, the town and its people. They would thus remain recorded forever, not only in Chagall's memory, but for the whole world to see.

Chagall had no home in Vitebsk at the time and moved from one room to another. Wherever he went, he took his paints and brushes and worked. He did paintings of his grandmother making jam, his father with a glass of tea at his side, one of his mother baking and one of her taking a nap; one of his brother David singing and playing the mandolin, and one of a sister dreaming at the window with a book in her hand. In addition, there are paintings of his many uncles—one in a barber shop, two of them having a discussion by a lamp. There are even paintings of his mother's little shop. There is a painting of an old man, with one white hand and one green; his sister Manya eating a bowl of soup; one of a wall clock, a newspaper delivery man; there are rabbis and religious, praying Jews, and acrobats. There are studies of children, of old men, of old women, of beggars. Then there are the landscapes of Vitebsk and its surroundings, its streets and its buildings. Also during this period, he painted a large number of self-portraits. Chagall recorded Vitebsk and its people, these first months after his return there, as few painters have ever depicted the life and times of any town or people.

In addition to his work, there was Bella, whom he loved more than ever and whom he was determined to marry. His newfound self-confidence, made firmer by the success of his exhibition in Berlin, had convinced him that he was ready to marry and able to provide for a wife—if the wife was Bella Rosenfeld.

The two young people had faithfully written to each other for four years. At the time Chagall returned to Vitebsk, Bella had just finished her studies at the Faculty of History and Philosophy in the Guerrier College for Girls in Moscow, the school she had studied at since the autumn of 1907. While there, she had also taken courses in drama under the famed director Konstantin Stanislavski. Of course, after four years, Chagall was a little worried before meeting Bella

From *My Life,* Plate 16, *The Wedding* (Drypoint)
The Art Institute of Chicago

again. Had she, perhaps, changed? There had been word, too, of some vague flirtation the beautiful girl had had with an actor in Moscow. Was this serious?

When the two met again, however, it was as if nothing had ever happened, as if they had never been separated. "The actor?" Chagall asked.

"Nothing," Bella replied, and neither one could hold back the tears of joy.

While Chagall worked hard on his series of Vitebsk documents, Bella brought food, day and night, to his studio. One day it would be sweet cakes; another, boiled milk and fish. She brought him decorative materials, and, once, even some boards he could use as an easel. More than food, however, she brought him inspiration and love. Through her, he learned to paint love with a tenderness and beauty few painters have equalled. These paintings are magical—the lovers are starry-eyed and seem transported in the skies by their newfound joy.

One of the finest of these is the painting called *The Birthday*. In her autobiography, written years later, Bella Chagall describes the afternoon on which the picture was painted. It was in July, 1915, Chagall's birthday. Bella came to his room bringing flowers with her, a lovely many-colored bouquet. Writing in her book to Marc Chagall, she says: "You test the brushes and pour paints—red, blue, white, black. You drag me into the stream of colors. Suddenly, you lift me from the ground and you yourself push off with one foot as though the small room has become too narrow for you. You take a leap, stretch to your full length, and fly up to the ceiling itself. Your head is turned and you turn mine as well. You creep behind my ear and whisper something. . . ."

Bella Rosenfeld and Marc Chagall would be married; the determined girl had succeeded in getting permission from her parents. However, it hadn't been easy, and the family was far from happy about their Bella's choice. After all, Marc's father worked in a herring warehouse. He wasn't even a clerk, though that would have been bad enough. On the other hand, Mr. Rosenfeld had three jewelry shops. In Bella's home, they ate enormous apple cakes, cheese cakes, while at Marc's home. . . . Papa Rosenfeld ate grapes; Papa Chagall, onions. Chicken was an ordinary meal for the Rosenfelds; the Chagalls were lucky to have it once a year.

Family, friends of family, they all rained words on Bella:

"It looks to me as though he puts rouge on his cheeks. What sort of husband will he make, that boy as pink-cheeked as a girl?"

"He'll never know how to make a living. You'll starve with him; you'll starve for nothing."

The Flying Fish
Albright-Knox Art Gallery, Buffalo, New York

Cow with a Parasol   Mr. Richard S. Zeisler, New York

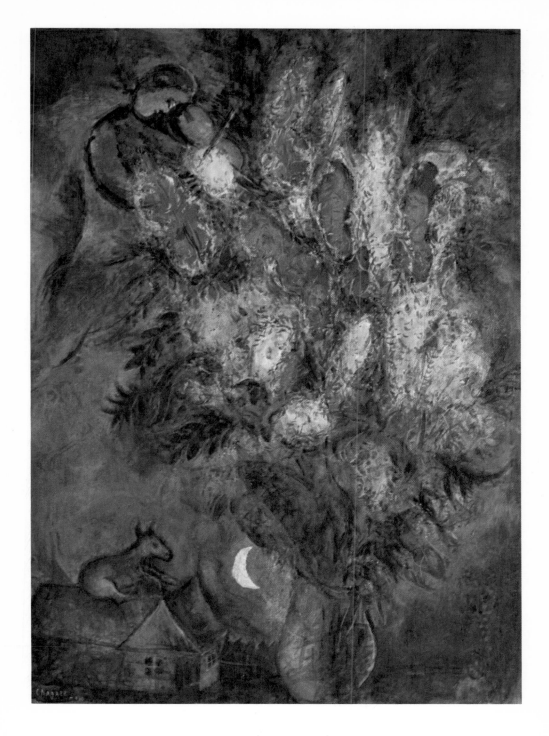

Vase of Flowers, at Night (1943)
Mr. and Mrs. Leo Glass, New York

Mariage Hivernal (Winter Marriage)
Perls Galleries, New York

"He's an artist. What does that mean?"

"And what will everyone say?"

But Bella knew who Marc was and what he was; and that she must be his wife. The wedding was planned; an elaborate one, of course, because of the Rosenfelds' position in the town. No expense was to be spared. Marc's poor father, ashamed to be among all those wealthy people who would attend, didn't even want to go, but his son pleaded with him to do so.

The date was set—July 25, 1915. Marc arrived very late at the Rosenfeld home. The rabbi and all the guests were waiting impatiently, but that didn't matter to Marc; all he cared about was his Bella. As he passed his way through the guests, they looked at him with embarrassment, and it was not too difficult for him to hear their comments:

"Yes, he's an artist."

"He's famous already, you know. He gets money for his pictures."

"It's still no way to earn a living."

"What about the fame and honor?"

"But, after all, who is his father?"

"Ah . . . I know."

Marc turned pale; he was ill at ease in this crowd of relatives, friends, and acquaintances, sitting, standing, and running about. He couldn't even enjoy the grapes and fruits and all the marvelous foods around them.

Before too long the ceremony—a beautiful, traditional one—began. His Bella was beside him, and he gained strength by tightly squeezing her hand. She was his . . . his wife.

Several hours later, they were in the country, in the little village of Zaolcha, not very far from Vitebsk. They were together, and they had what they wanted—woods, pines, quiet. The moon was shining behind the forest, a healthy pig was in the stable, and a horse was neighing outside the window, in the fields.

And the sky was lilac-colored.

WAR AND REVOLUTION

The marriage had taken place just a year after Chagall had returned from Paris. The newlyweds remained in the country until September. It was, Chagall has said, not a honeymoon as much as a milkmoon, for his wife fed him the good country milk.

In August he tried to get permission to go back to Paris with his bride. Application was made to the governor of the town, but to no avail. It was out of the question, for the war was on. In addition, he had to be concerned with military service. Because he was a painter, he asked to be placed in the camouflage service, but he was rejected. Fortunately, Bella's brother, Jacov Rosenfeld, was in charge of the war economy office in St. Petersburg; service in that office exempted one from a soldier's life, and Jacov was an important and successful lawyer, a man most suited to the manpower problems involved in the war economy office. But Marc, an artist, was not much good as an office worker. Facts and figures and statistics didn't interest him, and his brother-in-law was constantly bawling him out. He was given only minor jobs.

Living conditions were far from good at the time. Bella and Marc moved into one room after another; for a while they had to live in a dentist's home where snow fell in through the window and onto the bed. But his office job, though tedious, enabled him to meet a new circle of Russian intellectuals, with whom he was able to discuss the world of art. He also met, at the time, the art collector Kagan-Shabshay, who was the first to build up a considerable collection of Chagall's paintings.

Since his return from Paris, too, Chagall had had a chance to exhibit his work in Russia. In 1915, twenty-five of his works were shown in an important exhibition in Moscow. And in 1916 and 1917, important exhibitions of his work were held in St. Petersburg at the Dobitchina Gallery. His reputation was growing, and he was already known as one of the leading young artists of Russia.

The scope of his art was increasing with each new experience. Much time was spent during this period at a dacha in the country, and country scenes become a theme of his paintings. In 1916, a daughter, Ida, was born—a beautiful child who became the inspiration for some of the artist's most tender works. Then, too, the war, and soldiers—tired, worn out, anguished—entered into his work.

This was a period of the greatest upheaval in Russia. The Revolution came and with it the promise of a new life for the Jews of Russia. For many, many years they had been forced to live under heartbreaking and harsh restrictions. They were only able to live in certain sections of specified towns, and the fields in which they were able to work were severely limited as well.

The time was one of great excitement for the intellectuals and artists. They gathered about, discussed the new world to come, and made daring plans for the future. There was, perhaps, to be a new ministry of culture, and there was talk of Chagall becoming the Minister of Fine Arts. Bella, however, was strongly against such serious political involvement for the sensitive painter. She felt too that he could not work best in St. Petersburg, amidst the chaos caused by the Revolution and, at her urging, Chagall took his wife and baby daughter back to Vitebsk. They stayed at the home of Bella's parents. "This is my town and my tomb," he wrote to a friend in St. Petersburg.

In spite of Bella's fears that any political or administrative activities would do damage to Marc's painting, Chagall was appointed Commissar for Art in Vitebsk. In the difficult and confusing post-revolutionary days, it was a challenge: to remake his town into a great art center. He was to be director of a School of Fine Arts; he was also in charge of organizing exhibitions, setting up museums, and planning a program of lectures on art.

He threw himself into this work with his usual passion and enthusiasm. Even before he was officially appointed to his position, he had organized an exhibition of Vitebsk artists. He gave the place of honor to his former teacher, Pen; and he saw to it that paintings by the old friend from whom he had parted, Victor Mekler, were shown.

His big chance to show Russia how important Vitebsk was came on November 6, 1918, the first anniversary of the Revolution. There were to be huge celebrations in St. Petersburg and in Moscow; it was an occasion for Chagall to show just what the artists of Vitebsk could do. And, for Chagall, Vitebsk was a town full of artists—even the house painters were called to service to make this the biggest, brightest celebration possible. Sign painters and house painters—all were to put aside their ordinary work in order to contribute to the celebration.

For the big day, Vitebsk was a changed town. More than 350 banners were gaily decorated; all shops and trolleys were newly painted. Hundreds of flags flew in the wind, seven bright and gay triumphal arches were constructed, and stands for the public were erected. Never before had the town on the Dvina been so wildly and joyously decorated. Art, as Chagall had wanted, was brought down to the street. The artists were excited and exhilarated; and the man who had led this triumphant, joyous ceremony took pride in the smiles on the faces of the workers as they marched through the streets singing.

But the official reaction was something different. The leaders of the Communist Party were annoyed: Why is the cow green, and why is the horse flying in the sky? What did all this frivolity have to do with Marx and Lenin, with the Revolution? They even noted how many sets of underwear could have been made with the material they felt had been wasted on the flags and banners.

Chagall had known from the start that he could no more accept communism than he had been able to accept any ism—artistic or political. But it didn't matter. He set to work enthusiastically on the task of building up Vitebsk as a glorious art center. He would lead the artists towards what he considered "revolutionary art."

Times were hard, and there was the constant fight to get funds for the new Vitebsk museum and the art academy that he was to organize. This meant meetings, travels, it meant pleading with leaders who really didn't understand

his fire and his goals. Over a period of a few years, he succeeded in setting up the museum, but his greatest interest
was in his academy. It was there that he would take the
youngsters of Vitebsk and turn them into creative geniuses.
But he needed money—for paints, for materials, for class-
room equipment. When he left Vitebsk to travel about the
country in his quest for funds, Bella would replace him at
the school. He did obtain the money, but not without endless
battles and frustrations—there were always objections. Once,
he was asked whether he didn't feel it more important that
funds be allocated to rebuilding the bridge in the town than
to spending the money for an art school.

He persevered, built the school, traveled about Russia
to get the best possible teachers for the school. It was his
pride and joy, and he devoted many long hours to his administrative duties, often neglecting his own painting in order
to bring glory to Vitebsk. Dressed in a Russian blouse, with
a leather case under his arm, he was a director, an adminis-
trator. Only a few spots of pink on his cheeks, that had rub-
bed off from his paintings, revealed him as a painter. He was
loved and respected, and an amusing slogan was to be heard
in the school: "God grant that everyone may *chagalle* like
Marc Chagall." (The word *chagalle* in Russian means "march
forward.")

The school expanded rapidly under his energetic leader-

128

ship. Evening classes were started for those who could not attend during the daytime. Trips to the countryside were organized for the young painters, so that they might paint from nature. An art club was established, and a library of art books was put together.

It was a time of vitality and enthusiasm. But not everyone was as enthusiastic as Chagall and his followers. Party officials were opposed to the type of painting encouraged at the school. They wanted realistic art, art that easily and recognizably depicted the life of the people and the country, clear and simple illustrations. There was growing dissension in the school as well, and the teachers were divided in their attitudes toward painting. It was a battle between Chagall's group and the group that backed what they called "Suprematist Art." One day, when Chagall returned from one of his many fund-raising trips to Moscow, he found that the sign over the door of the academy had been changed: what had once read Free Academy was now Suprematist Academy. He immediately sent in his resignation. Most of the students rallied to his side. They knew the school could not grow and flourish without him, and they drew up a petition calling him the "sole moral support of the Academy." But Chagall was angry and hurt. He had given up his painting, his work, his time. The teachers that he had brought from all over Russia, the people he had helped so generously, were

129

the very ones who had revolted against him. Disgusted, he left for Moscow. A short time later, he gave in to the pleas of his supporters and returned to Vitebsk. But not for long. Within a few months, he left Vitebsk—for the last time— to go to Moscow.

The experience as the Vitebsk Commissar had been a good one and an interesting one, though in the end it proved frustrating. It was once again clear that Marc Chagall had to maintain an independent course. Although, because of the pressures of his administrative duties, he had been able to paint less than he wanted to, he did produce works of outstanding quality during the period. And in 1919, recognition came to him. At the first State Exhibition of Revolutionary Art, held in St. Petersburg, two rooms were devoted to his highly praised work.

Among the paintings just preceding this period was one called *The Green Violinist;* Chagall was to do several variations on this theme. It is dominated by a huge fiddler, playing his orange and yellow fiddle while one foot rests on a brown rooftop and the other on a gray one. His shoes are of different colors. His costume and his cap are violet, while his face is greenish-blue. He is in a sitting position, but it's impossible to tell just what he's sitting on. Above him, a few primitive houses and above them a violet-clad man floats in the clouds. The fiddler's face is crooked—the mouth goes

From *Dead Souls* by Gogol, Plate 72 (Etching and Drypoint)
The Art Institute of Chicago

off to one side, the nose to another. On the bottom left, an animal looks wistfully at the fiddler; on the right is a tree, a ladder against it and a bird on one of its bare branches. Everything seems to be moving, and the rhythm is unmistakable. The charm, beauty, and warmth of this painting have made it one of the most popular of all Chagall's work.

In May, 1920, Bella, Marc, and little Ida moved to Moscow. Because the painter had almost no money, the three had to live in one small, damp room. There were terrible food shortages, and it was often impossible to get milk for the little girl. Bella's once-wealthy family had been impoverished by the Revolution—the jewelry shops and all their money had been confiscated, so they were unable to help. Once, while trying to sell some of her own jewelry in order to raise money for the necessities of life, Bella had even been arrested by the police and held in jail for a while. In addition, word came from Vitebsk that both of Chagall's parents had died; he was not permitted to go to their funeral.

The most important creative experience for Chagall during these difficult days in Moscow came from the theater. In an attempt to rekindle Jewish culture at the time, a Jewish State Theater, under the direction of Alexis Granovsky, had been organized. Starting as a very small company in St. Petersburg, they moved to their own little theater in Moscow at the end of 1920, officially recognized as a State thea-

132

ter. Chagall had experimented with some designs for the theater while he was living in Vitebsk, and while there he had met Granovsky. In Moscow, Granovsky, at the suggestion of the art critic Efross, who had early recognized Chagall's genius, asked Chagall to help in designing sets for three short plays by the great Jewish author, Sholem Aleichem. He also asked Chagall to paint murals which would decorate the walls of the new little theater.

Chagall was delighted; he loved the theater and its special world. And he loved the stories of Sholem Aleichem, though he felt that, in presenting them too realistically and naturalistically on the stage, a disservice had been done to the great Jewish writer in the theater.

He feared that Granovsky would not give him the freedom he required, but he was wrong. The manager let him take over. Not only the sets, but the costumes, the movements, the makeup of the actors, everything was done a la mode Chagall. He worked hard and long hours; there was no money; he had to make do with the barest materials, the most inadequate equipment. By carefully supervising rehearsals, Chagall in a sense became the director. It was difficult for the actors to follow the style of their "director," but Chagall explained his interpretation of Sholem Aleichem and was able to convince the actors that what he wanted was correct for the play. Especially convinced was the leading actor, Mikhoels, who studied Chagall's paintings minutely until his every movement and gesture became attuned to that of Chagall's own figures. He was transformed by the artist.

On opening night, as the audience began to seat themselves on the benches, Chagall rushed about madly, touching up pieces of scenery, adjusting the costumes. His clothing was so covered with paint that he couldn't even appear in the auditorium.

But all his work had been worthwhile. The production of the three short plays was met with great enthusiasm. So were the murals, which Chagall had painted on canvas and then fastened onto the walls of the theater.

Soon an invitation came from the other Jewish theater, the Habimah, which was to perform one of the best known of all Jewish plays, Ansky's *The Dybbuk*. Chagall had met Ansky, who was also from Vitebsk, two years before, and the author had asked Chagall to work on a production of his play. Since Chagall admired *The Dybbuk*, he decided to accept the assignment in spite of the fact that the director of the Habimah, Wachtangoff, had been feuding with Granovsky. This collaboration, however, did not succeed. Chagall's anti-naturalism clashed with Wachtangoff's old-fashioned ideas of realism to such an extent that the painter walked off in a temper. He had to be free, he had to do his work in his own way. It was, certainly, some consolation for Chagall

134

to learn a year later that the manager of the Habimah had spent hours in front of his murals and then ordered another painter to paint in the style of Chagall.

Even with the success of the Sholem Aleichem plays, Chagall's life was a difficult one. There was no money— Granovsky was unable to pay. Bella and little Ida were living in the country near Moscow, and each evening, in his smock and wide trousers, Chagall would fight his way to get onto the crowded freight train that would take him to them. And the same thing each morning as he set out before dawn for his work.

In addition, his paintings were not selling as they had been. More and more the new regime turned against his modern and progressive work, and life in Russia seemed a constant frustration to the fiery, dedicated painter. For a short period, a new position did give him some satisfaction. In 1921, he was assigned to teach in a war orphans' colony near Moscow. Again there was no money and the artist was paid in food—rice, sugar, dried fish, even at times half a cow. But the experience of teaching the children was a beautiful one. They were all war orphans, many of whom had seen their parents brutally killed, been thrown out into the snowy streets, and had suffered every kind of pain and torture. They wandered about the city until some of them were finally taken in by the authorities and sent to children's shelters. The children lived in small houses, where they did all the work—cooking, baking bread, cutting and hauling firewood, and cleaning and mending. Barefoot, poorly clothed, they would come together for art lessons given by Chagall. They worked with tremendous enthusiasm and love for their teacher; and he felt the same for them. The children learned much from Chagall, who was also inspired by them.

In spite of his happiness in teaching these children,

From *Dead Souls* by Gogol, *The Arrival of Tchitchikov* (Etching)
Collection, The Museum of Modern Art, New York
Abby Aldrich Rockefeller Purchase Fund

Chagall was profoundly discouraged. He was a painter, and he had to paint. All doors seemed to be closed to him in Russia; he was not appreciated or understood. And the direction which the new government was taking would certainly not encourage his work any further.

He had left his prewar canvases in his beloved Paris and in Berlin. From the latter city a letter had come from his friend, the poet Rubiner, which said: "Are you alive? There is a rumor that you have been killed in the war. Do you realize you are famous here? Your pictures have introduced a new genre: expressionism. They're selling for high prices. Just the same, don't count on the money Walden owes you. He won't pay you for he maintains that glory is enough for you."

Chagall's mind was made up; he would return to Paris via Berlin. With the aid of friends, he obtained a passport and the money necessary to make the trip. He would always feel close to his mother country. But he wrote, "Neither Imperial Russia nor the Russia of the Soviets needs me. They don't understand me. I am a stranger to them."

He took the train to Berlin, and was never again to return to Russia. The Berlin Chagall came to in 1922 was quite different from the one he had left eight years before. It was a city in chaos, recovering from defeat in the war, going through a period of enormous economic inflation. The arts were flourishing: theater, music, and painting. It was, in addition, a kind of gateway to western Europe from the east—the Russian painters Archipenko and Kandinsky had already come here. And now Chagall. He was overjoyed to find that his friend Rubiner had been right; he was indeed famous in Berlin. Throughout the war, Walden had shown great courage in exhibiting his works and spreading his fame—after all, as a Russian, Chagall was the "enemy."

Chagall's first concern was to locate the paintings he had left with Walden in Berlin eight years before. He learned upon his arrival that Walden had been able to sell many of them to collectors; and since Walden had no idea of Chagall's whereabouts at the time, he deposited the monies received with a lawyer. When Chagall went to Walden to learn where the pictures were, the dealer refused to tell him. He merely offered him the sum of money that had been collected—a sum that because of inflation now meant almost nothing at all.

Chagall was bitter; somehow his past had been lost and there had not even been any financial compensation.

However, he stayed in Berlin for a year. His reputation was assured there, and in the German capital he was able to enter the main current of western art again. He made friends, visited the important artists and critics of the time, and had opportunities to exhibit his work. Most important,

138

he met Paul Cassirer, a publisher and gallery owner.

Cassirer had heard of an autobiography Chagall had been writing. Entitled *My Life,* it was started in 1911 when Chagall began jotting down impressions of his childhood. He had added to it while working in his brother-in-law's office in 1915-16 and had almost completed it during his last year in Russia when he felt a need to record his past. What Cassirer proposed was publication of this book along with twenty etchings to be executed by Chagall. The text itself was not published in German for many years, but Cassirer's offer gave Chagall his first opportunity to work in the medium of etching. Though Chagall painted little during his year in Berlin, his stay there was of great importance to him since it was there that he mastered this new technique of etching. Cassirer published the etchings—but not the book—in a portfolio. They were a great success, a brilliant start in a new medium.

PARIS AGAIN

In 1923, Chagall was back in his second birthplace. Paris seemed to him more marvelous than ever, and his heart leaped with joy as he wandered happily through its familiar streets. He knew he was home again.

Montparnasse was booming; there were new cafes, night clubs, and restaurants everywhere. At the cafes, the conversation had changed. Cubism had served its purpose and was dead. Dying too was the Dada movement, which had been founded in 1916 and was dedicated to the replacement of logical reason in art with deliberate madness and chaos. Surrealism—a movement in art and literature which stresses the uncontrolled imagination, pure fantasy, and the dream world—was being born.

Chagall, as soon as he arrived in the city, set out to

find his old friends. Apollinaire and Modigliani were dead, but still there were Lipschitz, Soutine, and above all, his dear friend Blaise Cendrars.

Cendrars had written to Chagall while the latter was in Berlin, telling him that he was famous in Paris and that the important dealer and publisher Ambroise Vollard had seen his paintings in the apartment of a critic, Gustave Coquiot, and wanted to meet him. Chagall well remembered having passed by Vollard's shop the first time he had come to Paris, many years before. Looking in the window, he had seen the fearful figure of the great Vollard, the man who had befriended the outstanding artists of the time and the man who had given Cézanne his first important exhibition. And then Chagall had lost courage, and had not entered the gallery. Now things were different. Vollard greeted him warmly and asked him to illustrate one of the greatest of all Russian novels, Gogol's *Dead Souls*. Price was no object—Vollard was willing to pay whatever the painter wanted. Chagall was overjoyed; he loved Gogol's book and, in addition, the dealer's offer freed him from all financial worries. No longer would he live on a piece of bread and a cup of coffee per day; more than that, he would be able to provide for his wife and daughter. The work fascinated him, too. Over a period of three years, he was to work on 107 full-page etchings, which constitute some of his finest work.

In these brilliant etchings, Chagall manages to capture all of the humor, sadness, and wisdom of Russian peasant life. Though Vollard never lived to see actual publication of the book, it was later published and remains one of the great illustrated books of all time, a rare example of a brilliant publisher's idea carried out just as brilliantly by the artist.

With renewed optimism, Chagall, Bella, and little Ida moved into a large studio apartment, with enough space for the painter to get back to work on his larger canvases. At first he was largely occupied with recapturing and actually repainting some of his earlier pictures. The reason for this was a sad one, quite simply that a large part of his output was no longer in his sight. He was well known and admired, but he actually owned little of his own work. Many of his paintings were in Germany; several had been left behind in Russia. Worst of all, he discovered that the more than 150 paintings which he had left behind at La Ruche were missing. After a patient search, he was able to trace some of them—which had been bought—but it was obvious that many had been either lost or destroyed. Because of this, he felt the need to reconstruct the past by redoing much of his earlier work—from copies or from memory.

Most important of all, however, Chagall was happy to be back in Paris, and to show the city and its beauties to Bella. With her, the excitement and the joy were doubled

142

—because they were shared. Paris remained the meeting place for the artists of the world; it was the city that could best give Chagall a chance to work and to show his work. Thus, the years between 1923 and the outbreak of World War II were to be, for the most part, the happiest of his life.

During this period, his art was to flourish as never before. Surrealism was the major topic of conversation, and Chagall felt much in common with its aims. The surrealists, too, felt that Chagall, who in many ways preceded them, should join their movement, and one day, three of their leaders—the German painter Max Ernst, the French poet Paul Eluard, and Gala, who became the wife of Salvador Dali, the painter—literally got on their knees to beg the Russian painter to join them. But once again Chagall felt he could never become part of any formal group. Just as he had rejected the communists politically and the cubists artistically, he rejected the pleas of the surrealists. He was Marc Chagall, and he had to go his own way.

His own horizons broadened during these years in France. He found inspiration not only in Paris, but in the vast and varied French countryside, the countryside which has inspired so many great painters. He and Bella and Ida traveled whenever possible—from the rugged, powerful Alps to the violent, rolling hills of the Mediterranean south. They

From *Fables* by La Fontaine, *The Fox and the Stork* (Etching)
Collection, The Museum of Modern Art, New York, Larry Aldrich Fund

grew to love the entire country as only new citizens can. Soon the effects of this love were shown in his paintings. Never before had he painted nature with such poetry, compassion, and light. There are color-splashed flowers, brilliantly varied landscapes, rich blue seas. From his stay at a charming, isolated village, Montchauvet, he was inspired to paint scenes of rural life, with cows, pigs, and poultry. Nature in all its varied forms became magical through Chagall's brush.

It is probably because of Chagall's love of the country and its animals that Vollard gave him his next commission —to illustrate the *Fables* of La Fontaine. These fables, written at the end of the seventeenth century, are among the great masterpieces of French literature. They are affectionate tales, often with a moral, of the tribulations of crows, mice, ants, and the like. They are graceful, beautifully told tales. Chagall and La Fontaine seemed a perfect combination—to Vollard and to Chagall himself, who was delighted. But much of the French public was horrified, and the subject was even debated in France's Chamber of Deputies. How could Marc Chagall, a Russian, an Easterner, be entrusted to illustrate one of the great works of French literature! Ignored was the fact that most of the tales which La Fontaine told had been adapted from Eastern sources; ignored too was the realization that Chagall's genius was universal.

145

Marc Chagall, Bella, and Ida, Paris, 1933
Photo by André Kertész

Vollard and Chagall were vindicated; the illustrations were
a great success, proving that Chagall was as capable of trans-
lating into pictures a French classic as he had been of illustrat-
ing a classic of his native land, *Dead Souls*.

Though Chagall continued, as always, to work hard,
he seemed to enjoy a richer and happier social life than ever
before. He and Vollard became good friends, and through

146

the dealer, he came to know the most important figures in the Parisian art world, among them Georges Rouault, a painter who was a master of religious subjects; Aristide Maillol, the sculptor; and Maurice Vlaminck, best known for his stormy landscapes. Chagall kept in close touch with the Russians in Paris as well and, from time to time, friends from his past would come to visit. Granovsky and his company performed for a while, and the Chagalls went to the theater almost every night. The actor Mikhoels spent much time in Paris, a good deal of it with Chagall. Diaghilev's ballets continued to have success, and the impresario always held seats in the theater for the Chagalls. Then there was Max Vinaver, exiled in Paris, a man to whom Chagall always remained grateful.

In every way, Chagall had found himself. With Bella at his side, in the country he loved, his art grew as never before.

In 1930, while Chagall was finishing his work on the *Fables,* Vollard and the painter agreed upon the next work to be illustrated: it would be the Bible. For such an enormous task, Chagall felt a visit to Palestine essential. The Bible had been significant in Chagall's life since his early days in the cheder. Abraham, Jacob, Moses, and David—all had become a part of his life. For this reason, Vollard felt the trip unnecessary, but to Chagall the trip to the actual land of the Bible was important.

In February, 1931, he boarded the S.S. *Champollion* with his wife and daughter; the ship was to take them to Beirut, from which the journey continued by land. On board the ship, Chagall had a chance to know the important Hebrew writer Chaim Bialik and the Swiss Jew, Edmond Fleg, a well-known poet, critic, and playwright. Because of this, the trip itself was a particularly interesting one.

But the arrival in Palestine—now Israel—went far beyond Chagall's greatest hopes. Met at the station in Tel Aviv by the Zionist leader and founder of Tel Aviv, Meier Dizengoff, he was soon to be totally captivated by the Biblical land of his dreams, a land to be transformed into a homeland for the exiled and homeless Jews of the world. The past, present, and future mingled together as one. In Israel, Chagall rediscovered the faces and traditions of his own past in Vitebsk, and he basked in the light of the land. He traveled enthusiastically throughout the country—Haifa, Jerusalem, Safed—visiting Rachel's tomb, the Wailing Wall, and the many synagogues. The rocky, age-old landscapes thrilled him, and he often painted out of doors. It was an exhilarating experience for the painter and for the man.

When he returned to Paris after three months, strengthened and enriched by all he had seen and felt, he began work on the Biblical etchings. He was to work on them for many years, and the entire work was not completed until 1956. It is one of the great inspirational works of art of our time, of all times.

During the 1930's, the Chagalls did a great deal of traveling outside of France. Though none of it matched his experience in Israel, the contacts with the masterpieces of other lands helped broaden Chagall's art. In 1932, a trip to Holland for the opening of one of his own exhibitions enabled him to study the paintings and etchings of Rembrandt. He stood spellbound before them, and they greatly influenced his etchings for the Bible. On a trip to Spain in 1934, he was moved by the Spanish masters—Velazquez, Goya, and, above all, El Greco, the Greek-born painter of mystic saints and profoundly religious scenes. In 1937, the Chagalls went to Italy where the painter was especially impressed by the works in the two great galleries of Florence— the Pitti and the Uffizi.

As with all great creative artists, Chagall drew inspiration from the works of other masters. For this reason, these trips to Holland, Spain, and Italy were of much significance. However, a trip to Poland in 1935 had special meaning for the painter. Invited there for the inauguration of the Jewish Institute in Vilna, he eagerly accepted, for he felt it would give him a chance to be near his native Vitebsk. Though he never did return to the town of his birth, in Vilna he once again came into contact with the life of eastern European Jews. Deeply saddened by what he felt was an ever-increasing threat to these people and by the concrete evidence of anti-Semitism, he made every effort to depict through his paintings scenes of a life he knew was disappearing. Though he himself was by now removed from the way of life of his youth, he desperately wanted to preserve on canvas this record of the past. A new tragic element was to enter his work.

WAR AND EXILE

On September 1, 1939, German troops invaded Poland, beginning World War II. Two days later, England and France declared war on Germany. An all-out effort had to be made to stop the aggression of Hitler's Germany, which threatened to overrun all of Europe. It was a period of fear and of chaos for all of Europe, but it was also a period marked by a determination to end the Nazi dictator's mad drive for power. On September 17, Poland was invaded by Russian troops, and less than two weeks later the country was divided between Germany and Russia.

Chagall was noticeably depressed. He had lived through war and revolution, and he knew the destruction they wrought. The fall of free Spain to the dictatorship of Generalissimo Franco had been a symbol of what was to come, and already in August of 1939 the Chagalls gathered up the painter's work and moved to Saint-Dye-sur-Loire, a small town away from Paris.

By the spring of 1940, the situation had worsened. Denmark and Norway, soon to be followed by Belgium, the Netherlands, and Luxembourg, were invaded by the German armies. It was obvious that the battlefield would move to France; the area near the Chagall home would most probably be a major line of defense for the French forces. It was thus necessary for them to move once again, this time to the south.

At Easter, Chagall and Bella drove to Gordes, an enchanting town in Provence, not too far from Avignon. Situated on a steep and rocky hillside, it commands a breathtaking view of the valley and surrounding mountains. It was there that they decided to settle, and they were fortunate to find a large, comfortable home—ideal for a studio as well—that had formerly been a Catholic girls' school. On May 10, the day the Germans invaded Belgium, the Netherlands, and Luxembourg, they bought the house.

The fall of France was imminent. On June 4, the British soldiers who had joined in the defense of France withdrew. More than 215,000 British troops, joined by 120,000 French, crossed the Channel from Dunkirk, heading for England in small boats. It was one of the most heroic and dramatic episodes of World War II.

Clown with Violin (1956)
Mr. and Mrs. Nate H. Sherman, Chicago

The Clown on the White Horse
Mr. E. W. Mudge, Jr., Dallas, Texas

Aleko (Setting for Act III)   Museum of Modern Art, New York

Installing Marc Chagall's Jerusalem Windows   David Rubinger photo

On June 14, the German army occupied Paris. The great city, the symbol of freedom, was to remain in Nazi hands for more than four years.

On June 22, France surrendered.

It was a black period for France and for the whole free world; and it was a dangerous one for all Jews, including the Chagalls. The Jews had been the prime targets of Hitler's madness. Their cities and villages were destroyed throughout Europe. The almost incredible number of six million of them were to be killed in Nazi concentration camps and torture chambers. Hitler was committing the greatest crime against humanity in the history of the world. No European Jew was safe; nonetheless, the Chagalls, hopeful that the tide of the war would change, that France would drive out the enemy, remained in Gordes for almost a year.

In the winter following their move there, a huge American car entered the small Provencal village. In it were Varian Fry, the American director of the Emergency Rescue Committee, which was doing its best to bring the leading European intellectuals to safety in America, and Harry Bingham, the American consul general in Marseille. They brought with them an invitation, from the Museum of Modern Art in New York, to the Chagalls to come to the United States. The museum also invited other important painters, such as Picasso, Dufy, Rouault, and Max Ernst.

Chagall was bewildered. He had never been to America, and it was so far away. "Are there trees and cows in America too?" he asked Fry.

Fry assured him that there were, but Chagall was still unconvinced of the need to leave his beloved France. He was grateful for himself and for all that America had been doing to shelter Jewish refugees, but he refused the invitation.

In April, however, after France had adopted strict anti-Semitic laws, he changed his mind. It was necessary to leave; as a Jew his life and that of his wife and daughter were threatened. It was a difficult moment when he, Bella, and Ida closed the house and traveled to the port of Marseille, from which they would begin the journey to America. But the potential danger of remaining in France was made clear even before they left, for Chagall was arrested and freed only after the intervention of Fry and Bingham. Because the United States was not yet at war, the American consul general still did retain some influence. And through New York's Museum of Modern Art, which gave as an excuse a possible exhibition of the painter's work, those paintings Chagall had in his possession were also allowed to be sent to America.

On May 7, 1941, Bella, Ida, and Marc Chagall, tired, weary, and frightened, began the long journey to America.

162

AMERICA

The United States was the haven of safety for refugees from all over the world during World War II. It opened its arms to persecuted Jew and non-Jew alike, as no other nation in history has done, to protect those who were threatened by Nazism. Just as it offered hope and a home to those driven from their own countries, so it received from them in turn an enormous contribution in the arts and sciences. Countless men, women, and children, fleeing from death or persecution, entered the harbor of New York during the years preceding and the early years of World War II. Many of them left distinguished marks on their second homeland; we have only to mention Albert Einstein and Arturo Toscanini, the latter not a Jew but an Italian seeking escape from Fascism.

So it was that Marc Chagall, his wife, and his daughter arrived in New York on June 23, 1941. It was a significant date for the painter, for only the day before the Germans had invaded his first home, Russia.

When the Chagalls arrived, the United States was still not at war; but war was obviously imminent and less than a month before President Roosevelt had proclaimed a state of national emergency. The New York of 1941 was different from that of today. There was no television, and no jets flew over the city. William Shirer's *Berlin Diary,* published recently, had documented the rise and peril of Nazi Germany. But America was still playing. On Broadway, some of the biggest hits of the American theater were running: *Life with Father, The Man Who Came to Dinner, Pal Joey, Arsenic and Old Lace,* and *The Corn is Green.* Bob Hope's new film, *Caught in the Draft,* with its comic military background, was a hit. Ty Cobb and Babe Ruth, baseball immortals, were playing golf together. And *Captain Midnight* was a popular radio serial.

Chagall was at first overwhelmed by New York; the grandeur of the great metropolis, its skyscrapers, and its tempo frightened him. He felt himself a man without a country and without a language. He knew no English, and few New Yorkers spoke French. He had once again been uprooted by events of history. Fortunately, his work was well

164

known in America—he had won the important Carnegie Prize in 1939—and he was warmly greeted upon his arrival both by members of the American art world and by those old friends who had also sought refuge in the United States.

Soon after their arrival, the Chagalls found an apartment, not far from Central Park, and their home became a gathering place for fellow artists and refugees from Europe. This helped raise his spirits. Having brought many pictures with him that he had been working on for years, he settled down to work again as soon as possible.

Chagall's first major work in America began in 1942, when the New York Ballet Theater, one of America's best ballet companies, commissioned him to design the scenery and costumes for a new production of *Aleko,* to be choreographed by the famous Russian, Leonide Massine. The story was based on a poem, "The Gypsy," by Russia's greatest poet, Aleksander Pushkin; and the ballet was to be danced to a piano trio by Tchaikovsky. It was an ideal collaboration; two Russians, working in America, with the themes and music of their mother country. In a way, two great artists, in recreating their homeland from memory, were also making a special home for themselves among the towering skyscrapers of New York. Day after day, Chagall and Massine worked closely together, the melodious strains of Tchaikovsky recordings in the background. Chagall was not content to paint alone; his ideas included choreographic movement as well as set and costume design.

For technical reasons, the Ballet Theater decided to give the first performance of *Aleko* in Mexico City in September (the first New York performance took place at the Metropolitan Opera House on October 6, 1942). Thus, as soon as the preliminary work was finished, the Chagalls and Massine left for the Mexican capital. It was August when they arrived, and the painter was immediately heartened by the warmth and generosity of the country and its people; its rich colors reminded him of the Mediterranean. Unfortunately, in the month that preceded the first performance, there was little time for anything but work. Chagall took charge of each element of the production. No detail, no minor prop escaped his careful attention. Bella was an enormous help, as always. She organized a studio in the theater itself, found Mexicans to help her, and supervised the difficult making of the costumes, many of which required hand-painting. All the while, Chagall worked, painting four huge backdrops by himself, rarely leaving the theater. It was an exciting and exhilarating experience—working among people he loved, in a country he could feel close to, and once again in the theater, where he was able to express his own profound love for ballet, painting, and music.

The premiere took place on September 10.

166

The Mexican audience had been cool to most of the ballets performed by the American company throughout the season. Then the curtain went up on *Aleko*. Briefly, it is the tragic story of a young man who flees from civilization to join a gypsy camp. There he falls in love with the daughter of the chief, but he soon learns that she loves another man. The young man, Aleko, is desperate; he finds the girl and her lover and kills them both. For this, he is rejected by the gypsies, who break up their camp, leaving Aleko alone, weeping on the grave of the girl and her lover.

Chagall did one backdrop for each of the four acts. The first represents love. It is a moonlit night. We can see a lake, a red cock, lovers emerging from the sky, and faintly visible, the gypsy tents. The second backdrop has as its motif the harvesttime; there is the sun, a floating branch of a tree, a field, flowers, and a scythe. The third is a dream—sprawling hillside village, a large bouquet of flowers with a monkey hanging by its tail from it, and on the ground, a dancing bear, fiddle and bow in hand. The final backdrop shows city life, with city buildings separated by roads, all of them red. In one corner, on a hill, is a green cemetery. In the sky is a large gold sun, burning candles on its face; toward it runs a white horse, which takes up the whole center of the sky.

The audience was enchanted. Music, poetry, movement, and color had been combined into a glowing whole. Time and again, Chagall was called back to acknowledge the cheers of the Mexican public. It was in every way a triumph.

Once back in New York, Chagall's work showed the influence of the Mexican colors and light. In addition, because of news of the war in Russia and Russia's valiant fight against the German army, reports from his motherland were frequent, and the painter's work showed a strong Russian influence. He was worried and saddened by the threat to the world in which he grew up, and this concern is reflected in his work.

The Chagalls stayed in New York, but spent a great deal of their time in the country. Weekends and months at a time were spent in areas close to New York. For the summer of 1944, they rented a house at Cranberry Lake, in the Adirondacks. It was there, on August 25, that they heard the joyous news of the liberation of Paris. The war was not yet won, but they now felt it would soon be, that they would soon be able to return to France.

In the midst of their elation over the news from Europe, personal tragedy struck. What seemed to the doctors at the hospital in Cranberry Lake a minor virus infection was in

The Artist's Wife (Etching and Drypoint)
The Art Institute of Chicago

168

fact an infection that was to take Bella's life on September 2.

Bella had somehow felt, when she and her husband and daughter were forced to leave Europe three years before, that her life was coming to an end. In fact, her last two years were busily spent writing her memoirs, which she had started putting on paper in 1935. At her untimely death, she had completed two volumes, one of which was published in English under the title *Burning Lights*. These memoirs, in their way, do for Vitebsk in words what Marc Chagall was able to do in color and form.

Bella's death was an enormous loss for Chagall. She had been his life, his world, and his grief is best expressed in the preface he wrote to her books:

> *For many years my art felt the influence of her love. But it seemed to me that something in her was being silenced, that something was being pushed aside.*
>
> *I felt that in Bella's heart lay treasures, dewy with love. . . .*
>
> *Her style . . . is the style of a Jewish bride in Yiddish literature. She wrote as she lived, as she loved, as she made friends. Her words and lines are like paint breathed upon a canvas. . . .*
>
> *Things, people, landscapes, Jewish holidays,*

170

flowers—this is her world and this is what she tells about. . . .

Towards the end I used to find her in the middle of the night, sitting in bed under a small lamp, reading Yiddish books. I used to say, "So late? Better go to sleep."

A few weeks before her last sleep—I see her still fresh and lovely as always at the room in our summer place. She spreads out her papers covered with writing. Here, finished pieces; here, sketches; and here, copies. So I ask her, hiding my fear, "Why such order suddenly?"

She answers with a pale smile, "This way you will know where and what everything is. . . ."

In her everything was deep and quiet intuition. I still see her from the hotel window as she sits at the edge of the pond, before going into the water. She waits for me. Everything in her is listening to something, as she listened to the forest long ago when she was a little girl.

I see her back, her thin profile. She doesn't move; she waits, thinks . . . And perhaps she already sees the "other world."

Her last words to me were: "My notebooks."

A loud clap of thunder and a burst of rain

171

broke out at six o'clock in the evening on the 2nd of September, 1944, when Bella left this world. Everything went dark before my eyes.

Marc and Bella Chagall had lived an unusually rich life together. Since he had first met her in Vitebsk, she had been a source of inspiration for his work. Through her, and because of his love for her, he was able to paint extraordinary pictures of couples in love—floating through the air, flying joyously through space, holding each other with profound love and happiness. Chagall has often been called a painter of love. If this is so, it is undoubtedly due in large part to the love he discovered with Bella.

For nine months after her death, Chagall was unable to paint. He spent his time in his studio, the pictures turned to the wall. He was inconsolable, and his time was spent helping his daughter Ida to translate Bella's autobiography, *Burning Lights,* into French. By doing that, he was still in some way with his beloved wife. When, after many months, he slowly began to paint again, all of his work reflected the grief he felt at the loss of his lifelong companion.

Perhaps the best opportunity to recover from his mood of depression and loneliness came in 1945 when the New York Ballet Theater asked him to design the scenery and costumes for their new production of *The Firebird,* a ballet based on an old Russian folktale. It was to be choreographed by Adolph Bohm, and the music was Igor Stravinsky's. Chagall eagerly accepted the assignment, for by working on a story of magic and pure fantasy, he might in some way escape from the reality of life without Bella. *The Firebird* was just such a tale, the story of a prince who frees (and finally marries) a princess by means of a magical golden feather he had been given by a firebird in gratitude for his having freed the captured bird one day. It is a rich and wondrous plot, well suited to Chagall's colorful imagination.

To work on the costumes and sets, he spent the summer of 1945 in the country surrounding New York; first on Beaver Lake in Ulster County and then at Sag Harbor on Long Island.

There was an enormous amount of work involved, just as there had been for *Aleko*. Sketches were made for about eighty costumes, which were executed in Chagall's studio under the constant supervision of Ida as well as that of the painter himself. In addition, Chagall painted a huge curtain and a backdrop for each of the ballet's three scenes.

The production, which opened in New York in October, 1945, was an immediate success, the audience enthralled from the moment the opening curtain, a huge flying figure of a half-girl, half-bird carrying a bouquet of flowers, was revealed. Applause filled the theater for each new backdrop: the first which showed an enchanted forest; the second, the palace of the magician where the princess is held prisoner; and the joyous third which represents the wedding feast. Once again, Chagall had demonstrated his total affinity for all the arts.

On May 7, 1945, Germany had unconditionally surrendered. The war in Europe had thus come to an end. Within a few more months, Japan too surrendered, and World War II was over. It was time for Chagall to start thinking of a return to France. He could hardly wait to see his beloved Paris again.

The following April, an important exhibition of his work took place at the Museum of Modern Art in New York. A month later, he returned to Paris for an emotion-filled visit. The city of light had been dimmed, but its enchantment remained.

In 1947, he returned to Paris again, this time for an exhibition of his work that inaugurated the new Musée National d'Art Moderne.

It wasn't until August, 1948, that Chagall returned to France for good. He was grateful for all America had done for him, but he was happy to be home.

His position as a painter was secure. Important exhibitions of his work were held throughout Europe—at the Tate

174

From *Dead Souls* by Gogol, Plate 55 (Etching and Drypoint)
The Art Institute of Chicago

Gallery in London, the Stedelijk Museum in Amsterdam, the Kunsthaus in Zurich, and the Kunsthalle in Berne. He was an important attraction at the Venice Biennale, Italy's semi-annual showing of major modern painting.

As always, he continued to work hard, perhaps harder than ever. Vollard had died in 1939, but in Teriade, a dedicated and brilliant publisher, Chagall found a worthy successor. It was Teriade who finally published *Dead Souls,* the *Fables,* and the etchings for the Bible. Chagall's interests expanded. Soon he was doing sculpture and ceramics. As time passed, his energies seemed to increase. His genius was boundless, striking out in every direction.

In 1950, he moved to a house in Vence, a small hilltop town not far from Nice. The house itself is called Les Collines (The Hills); Marcel Proust once stayed in it. The nearby studio, white like the house, was once used by Paul Valery, the great poet. Both are reached by climbing a long path, surrounded by grass, trees, and flowers. It is a beautiful enchanted garden, far from Vitebsk. There, among the fruits, flowers, and scents of the Mediterranean countryside, Chagall's art flourished. His colors became more brilliant than ever, as if soaked in the blue of the sky and the warmth of the sun.

In 1952, Chagall married Valentine (Vava) Brodsky, a charming woman with whom he has shared his life ever since. Together they have traveled extensively—to Italy, Greece, Israel, Denmark, and all over the United States. They have had a beautiful and a productive life. But in 1952, Chagall could not realize that perhaps his most exciting and important works were still to come.

176

THE GRANDEUR OF CHAGALL

After having seen a retrospective exhibition of Chagall's works at the Musée des Arts Décoratifs in Paris in 1959, Dr. Miriam Freund, president of Hadassah, a women's organization which has done so much to help the state of Israel, and Joseph Neufeld, a noted architect, had an idea. Neufeld had been asked to build a medical center for Hadassah, in the Judean hills five miles from Jerusalem. Part of the building would be a synagogue. To both Neufeld and Dr. Freund, Chagall seemed the perfect man to execute the stained glass windows.

Chagall was enthusiastic about the project, for the chance to work in a medium he found especially exciting at the time. In 1950, he had first thought about the possibilities of glass painting, at that time in connection with a

177

project for the Chapelle du Calvaire at Vence. This was not completed, but a few years later he was asked to decorate the baptistry of the church of Notre Dame de Toute Grâce, at Plateau d'Assy, a small French town in the province of Savoie. Part of the decoration included two small stained-glass windows; his work on these windows is delicate, with little use of color.

His second experience with stained glass came when the Administration of Historic Monuments invited him to design two large windows for the cathedral of Metz. He found the need to work with light itself particularly fascinating, and with more passion than ever, he began to master the techniques involved. He carefully studied the stained-glass windows at the great cathedral of Chartres, and set to work with Charles Marq, a highly-skilled glass craftsman from an old workshop in Reims, not far from Paris in the north of France. Their collaboration in working on the windows for Metz proved to be highly successful, though the work went slowly since the problems of transferring the painter's rich colors to glass were tremendous.

Though the design for both Metz windows had been completed, the actual work had been done on only one when

The Bible: *Crossing the Red Sea* (Etching)
Collection, The Museum of Modern Art, New York
Gift of Dr. Arthur Lejwa

Chagall was approached to work on the windows of the Hadassah hospital. Since this was to be a completely new building, unlike those at Plateau d'Assy and Metz, thus enabling the artist to have total freedom, he interrupted the work at Metz and eagerly threw himself into the work for the hospital.

There were to be twelve arched windows, more than ten feet high and eight feet wide. Each would represent a Tribe of Israel—Reuben, Simeon, Levi, Judah, Zebulun, Issachar, Dan, Gad, Asher, Naphtali, Joseph, and Benjamin —the twelve sons of Jacob, according to the Old Testament. Chagall was faced with the problem of the Second Commandment which forbids the portrayal of the human face; for this reason, these windows contain the figures of animals, fish, winged horses, and flowers, together with religious symbols, such as the Star of David, candlesticks, and the Tablets of the Law. Each of the twelve Biblical themes is depicted by means of these animals and symbols, by means of landscapes and towns and the sea, all with dazzlingly vibrating colors.

The Jerusalem windows are a work of genius, rightly considered the finest stained glass of modern times. Before their installation in Israel, the windows were exhibited in Paris and then in the United States to enormous, admiring crowds. In creating these masterpieces, Chagall had brilliantly overcome the problems of this difficult, painstaking technique, an art almost lost since the Middle Ages.

Perhaps Chagall's greatest honor to date came in 1962, when France's Minister of Cultural Affairs, André Malraux, himself a great novelist and art historian, commissioned Chagall to redecorate entirely the enormous ceiling of the magnificent Paris Opera house. This would be Chagall's gift to his beloved adopted country and for two years he worked on this project.

Often, as he worked on his elaborate sketches, the sound of Mozart, his favorite composer, came from his record player. This was to be his ultimate tribute to his love for music.

On September 23, 1964, twenty-one hundred invited guests filed into the great opera house. It was a gala, historic evening, for the new ceiling was to be unveiled. Tension mounted. Just as people had said, many years before, that the painter from Vitebsk could never illustrate the *Fables* of La Fontaine, France's great classic, so many were now saying that this painter could never successfully decorate the ceiling of one of France's national monuments.

As the audience began to enter the auditorium, the huge crystal chandelier which dominates the theater was dark; the new ceiling was not yet visible. The people took their seats, the music began, and there followed a gay procession of the entire *corps de ballet*. The dancers came to the front of the stage, and the enormous chandelier was lit. All heads turned upward. With joy and wonder the gala audience greeted the magnificent new crown that adorned their opera house, its brilliant colors shining down and casting a spell over the entire house. Then all heads turned toward the special box at the rear of the orchestra, for in it was the beaming Chagall, waving at the audience, acknowledging the thunderous applause, happily shaking hands with André Malraux. The celebration ended as the orchestra played the joyous last movement of Mozart's *Jupiter Symphony*.

The ceiling is indeed a triumph. Chagall conceived it as "a mirror" to reflect "in a bouquet of dreams the creations of the performers and composers." The entire work is like a flower with five petals. Each petallike section has a dominant color—blue, green, red, white, and yellow—and in each we find figures and symbols of the world of ballet and opera and their composers. "There is nothing precise in it," Chagall has said. "One cannot be precise and still be true." But in this huge circular painting we can make out a birdlike figure playing a flute, representing Mozart, and near this Czar Boris Godunov; and we can see two of opera and ballet's most famous lovers, Tristan and Isolde, and Romeo and Juliet. And amidst the warm, rich colors, we find the face of André Malraux, Chagall's personal tribute to the man who enabled him to enter more than ever before into the tradition and culture of France.

Major assignments in America were still to come, and, in 1966, Chagall was again to be associated with the Metropolitan Opera House. Twenty-four years before, his production of *Aleko* had been a great success at the Met. But that had been the old Met, which was now to be torn down and replaced by a new building in New York's Lincoln Center. For the grand foyer of this new building, Chagall was asked to execute two huge murals. Each is thirty-six feet tall and thirty feet wide; one is called "The Sources of Music," and the other is entitled "The Triumph of Music." They are an extraordinary demonstration of his passion for music. "The Sources of Music" is mainly yellow, while "The Triumph of Music" is predominantly red. Throughout both, figures of Chagall's past and present—including New York, seem to float. We see not only birds and flowers, lovers and winged animals, but we also find New York—part of Saint Patrick's Cathedral, the George Washington Bridge, and the city's skyline, all blended into visions of fantasy. As seen from the large plaza in front of the Metropolitan, they give a joyful greeting to the visitor approaching the opera house.

The Bible: *Joseph, The Shepherd* (Etching)
Collection, The Museum of Modern Art, New York
Gift of Harry C. Oppenheimer

For that inaugural season of New York's opera house, Chagall was also given another assignment—to design the sets and costumes for Mozart's opera, *The Magic Flute*. Here was his opportunity to pay personal homage to his favorite composer, but the challenge was enormous. *The Magic Flute* is a magnificent opera, an incredibly beautiful theatrical work written in the form of *Singspiel,* or German ballad opera. But its complicated plot—a mixture of mysticism and fantasy and Masonic lore—has always made it difficult to stage. Its settings include strange forests, Egyptian temples, mysterious caves, rugged mountains, a sacred grove, a subterranean temple, moonlit gardens, and for the finale, the Temple of the Sun. It is peopled by fantastic animals, half-human birds, a Queen of the Night, slaves, a High Priest, a Prince and a Princess, as well as others.

Since its first production in 1791, countless artists and designers have accepted the challenges of *The Magic Flute;* but very few have met them successfully. Chagall set to work. Month after month, day and night, he lived *The Magic Flute*. He became a part of Mozart's fantasy world, and Mozart became a part of his. Guided by his love for Mozart's music, his feeling of kinship with it, he soon became immersed in it.

Several weeks before the premiere, Chagall came to New York for the final preparations. New York had become, in a way, his third home. He had expressed his love for it in the Metropolitan Opera House murals; now he had to make certain that everything would be perfect for the production of his beloved *Magic Flute*. He threw himself into the job as he had done years before in the Russian theater, as he had done for the Ballet Theater. Indeed, because it is a world of make-believe, the world of the theater stimulated him.

On the night of February 19, 1967, Chagall was seated in a box at the Metropolitan Opera House as the curtain went up on *The Magic Flute*. What the viewers saw amazed them. Chagall had designed thirteen full curtains, each one about seventy feet high and forty feet wide. In addition, there were twenty-six partial curtains, and 120 separate costumes. As each new curtain came into view, the crowd applauded wildly. Every stage picture evoked frenzied enthusiasm. What the public saw was not the usual stage scenery, but a staggering number of Chagall pictures which, through their vibrant, brilliant colors and Mozartian symbolism brought to life the music of Mozart and added a commentary of their own. It was a dazzling production; even the costumes, one critic noted, "are Chagall paintings wrapped around people." As the curtain came down on the final scene, the scene of triumph which Chagall had painted in brilliant reds, it was clear that the occasion had been one of historic importance, that this production would remain one of the great operatic productions of our time.

The following morning, writing in his paper, a critic complained that there was too much Chagall and not enough Mozart. But the rest of the critics, as well as the public which fought to buy seats for the following performances, felt it was a triumph. Marc Chagall was the toast of New York. Though anxious to return home to begin work again, he agreed to remain in the city a few days so that the mayor could confer on him New York City's highest cultural honor, the Handel Medallion, to express the city's recognition of Chagall's artistic contributions to New York through his works at the Metropolitan, as well as the memorial glass panel which the artist had done for the United Nations. A gathering of New York's leading figures responded warmly as Chagall expressed his gratitude for the city's hospitality and refuge during the difficult days of World War II.

The next day Chagall left for his home in France. Much work was ahead of him, including another exciting assign-ment, for Gobelins in Paris, the most famous tapestry works in the world, were preparing his tapestries, depicting Old Testament scenes, to be hung in the Knesset, Israel's Parlia-ment.

Ahead of him too was life in a new house, at Saint-Paul-de-Vence, only a few miles from Vence. Nearby stands France's most beautiful new museum, the museum of the

Fondation Maeght. Some of the finest works of the great painters and sculptors of our time are shown there; significantly, an entire room is devoted to the works of Marc Chagall.

His life has been an extraordinary one, marked not only by genius but by a strong determination to remain faithful to his singular vision. His paintings need to be felt as well as seen. In recreating Vitebsk for us, he has given us a world; with his floating lovers, his fiddlers on the roof, and his flying cows, he has shown us love. His place in the history of art is unique and secure; through his work, he has enriched our lives.

FOR FURTHER READING

It is impossible to list all the books, newspapers, and magazine articles consulted in the preparation of this short biography. However, for those interested in knowing more about Chagall and his work, the following books are suggested: The painter's own early autobiography, *My Life* (New York: The Orion Press, 1960); Bella Chagall's charming and warm autobiographical volume, *Burning Lights* (New York: Schocken Books, reissued in 1962); Jean Cassou's poetic and sensitive study, *Marc Chagall* (New York: Frederick A. Praeger, 1965); and, finally, Franz Meyer's comprehensive, definitive work, *Marc Chagall* (New York: Harry N. Abrams, 1963).

LIST OF ILLUSTRATIONS

192